Life After ...
Business and
Administrative Studies

A practical guide to life after your degree

Sally Longson

Routledge
Taylor & Francis Group

LONDON AND NEW YORK

First published 2006
by Routledge
2 Park Square, Milton Park, Abingdon, Oxon OX14 4RN

Simultaneously published in the USA and Canada
by Routledge
270 Madison Ave, New York, NY 10016

Routledge is an imprint of the Taylor & Francis Group, an informa business

© 2006 Sally Longson

Typeset in Sabon by
HWA Text and Data Management, Tunbridge Wells
Printed and bound in Great Britain by
TJ International Ltd, Padstow, Cornwall

British Library Cataloguing in Publication Data
A catalogue record for this book is available from the British Library

Library of Congress Cataloging-in-Publication Data
Longson, Sally.
   Life after – business and administrative studies: a practical guide to
   life after your degree / Sally Longson.
      p.   cm.
   "Simultaneously published in the USA and Canada by Routledge."
   Includes bibliographical references and index.
      1. Business – Vocational guidance.   2. Management – Vocational
      guidance. 3. Business students – Employment   4. College graduates
      Vocational guidance   I. Title
   HF5381.L657 2006
   650.14–dc22   2005035073

ISBN10: 0–415–37591–6
ISBN10: 0–203–08841–7
ISBN13: 978–0–415–37591–7

Life A...
Busin...
Administra...

Thousands of students graduate from university each year. The lucky few have the rest of their lives mapped out in perfect detail – but for most, things are not nearly so simple. Armed with your hard-earned degree, the possibilities and career paths lying before you are limitless, and the number of choices you suddenly have to make can seem bewildering.

Life After ... Business and Administrative Studies has been written specifically to help students currently studying, or who have recently graduated, make informed choices about their future lives. It will be a source of invaluable advice and wisdom to business graduates, covering such topics as:

* Identifying a career path that interests you
* Seeking out an opportunity that matches your skills and aspirations
* Staying motivated and pursuing your goals
* Networking and self-promotion
* Making the transition from scholar to worker
* Putting the skills you developed at university to good use in life

The *Life After ...* series of books are more than simple 'career guides'. They are unique in taking a holistic approach to career advice – recognising the increasing view that, although a successful working life is vitally important, other factors can be just as essential to happiness and fulfilment. They are *the* indispensible handbooks for students considering their future direction in life.

Sally Longson is a life coach and well-known writer and media commentator in the field of care...

Also available from Sally Longson

Life After ... Art and Design
0-415-37590–8

Life After ... Engineering and Built Environment
0-415-37592-4

Life After ... Language and Literature
0-415-37593-2

Contents

Preface

You've done it – or you're on the way to it. Graduation Day. What a proud day for you and your loved ones! And everyone's asking you, 'What are you going to do now?' or 'What are you going to do next?'

Your degree over – or nearly over – you contemplate your next move, rather like a game of chess. You plot your next move, you fall into it, or someone makes you fall into it. Life is continually like a game of chess. You can plan your next few moves through a series of moves, or take them one move at a time, usually as opportunities occur – or you can become a pawn in body, mind and spirit, moved around a board at someone else's bidding. So take the initiative – as a graduate, you'll be well practised in doing just that – and plot your life and career with strategy to enhance control.

Life overall is much more competitive for all of us wherever we are, as we try to grab the attention of customers, clients, the boss, our team mates, our kids and friends. And yet the amazing and boundless opportunities which we could create through using our knowledge and imagination means that today, we can think the unthinkable, if we focus on finding the best way forward and on un-blocking those obstacles in our path. Unlock your creativity and put it to work, and you could come up with the next big earning website – you may have done so already. The range of businesses, charities and posts today mean there's a huge range of opportunities open to you which match your interests and passions. We can choose to be self-employed, employees, project managers, work on a temporary or contract basis, to travel when they please (some people find this part particularly hard to give up and are still finding themselves at it when they hit 50). We simply need to be innovative, creative, adaptable, flexible, courageous and ready to seize the moment with both hands. We need to open our eyes and zap the gaps in the market we see before someone else gets there first. In short, we can create our own opportunities.

Nonetheless, there are mixed messages with regards to the demand for graduates. Many countries in the Organisation for Economic Co-operation and Development (OECD) already have a participation rate in higher education of 60 per cent plus, including Australia, Finland, Hungary, Iceland, Poland, Norway and New Zealand. On the one hand, countries are pushing the numbers of graduates they produce up, up and up. On the other hand, too many graduates are taking on jobs for which a degree is not even required. They are, in effect, under-employed. There are those captains of industry who are phenomenally successful without having been to university, but also those graduates who emphasise the time they spent there were the best years of their life, and they wouldn't have missed it for the world. Each to their own.

You know that the global economy has led employers to outsource work to other parts of the world and form partnerships, alliances and mergers with others to give them a global stage. A company in China can buy one in the UK. Workers in India are the back-office for many UK companies. Many companies have branches throughout the world with one cross-organisational operating practice which nonetheless also takes local differences into account. Some form strategic alliances with other organisations of similar values and services in parts of the world they want to reach. The small company in Basingstoke, southern England, can capture a share of the market in Russia. The company in Nepal may pick up the services of a one-man band in Dijon. The practice of outsourcing work to freelances has opened up a whole new avenue of opportunities to those seeking self-employment. Don't limit your horizons to your home shores. Look out across the sea of opportunity before you and cast your mind and eyes beyond.

Having a degree does not guarantee having a good job. *Nothing* in life guarantees you a job. But there are key strategies you can enlist to enhance your chances of enjoying the career and life you want. And you may land yourself a job – but if you want a *great* job, then a major responsibility lies with you to make it so. Careers, like marriage and parenthood, need work and nurturing, and the hard work really only begins when you've started them. It is persistent hard work, but worth it.

On the plus side, the number of positions demanding higher skills is on the increase. The following figures show that the demand for skilled, educated people *is* on the up. In the UK for example, the numbers of mangers, senior officials, professional and associate professional technical workers is expected to rise. Employers need highly skilled people if they are to succeed and outperform their competitors. There is a huge difference in the quality of life and opportunity between those areas with highly skilled workers and the new industries; and those areas where there are low skill levels and outdated and rapidly disappearing sectors. The problem is that neither graduate nor small company knows where to start in getting together and how to make the most of each other. Neither knows enough about each other. Look out for graduates working for small or micro-businesses. Ask them questions. How did it happen? What do they do? Who did they know to get the role? Which organisations helped, if any? What initiatives are about to bring graduates and small or micro-businesses together? Many government agencies are spearheading huge regeneration projects in their poorer regions and working with universities and employers (small, medium and large) to ensure that graduates are retained in the area and that their skills and knowledge are well used.

Whether you're a student who's never had a year out of education in your life, or someone who went back to university for whatever reason after working for some years, now is a great time to assess your life ahead and what you want out of it. Let's get started!

Chapter 1

Decisions, decisions ...

What happens now? What happens next?

What happens from now on depends on how determined you are to bring your hopes and aspirations, dreams and ambitions to fruition. These may be very clear to you. Equally, you may be kicking lots of ideas about, or simply not have a clue. What you do know is that there are lots of decisions to make and plans to be laid – but what, exactly? Where do you start?

Looking at the next few months

If you've already left university, you may have happily spent the summer enjoying a break at home before considering what happens next. The start of the academic year may feel strange as you realise that for the first time, perhaps in your life, you do not have to go back to school, college or university. You're free to do as you like. And what's more, no one will notice or care what you do, apart from the people you live with, such as your parents. They aren't used to you being around and may start giving you odd jobs to do which interfere with your day and which you may resent. Meal times may be punctuated with discussions about your future and visitors to the house ask you about your plans. It may feel as though life is going backwards fast, instead of moving on to greater things. Build a structure around your life, even if you have no work or study to go to. Keeping to a routine will help you when you start work.

You may have studied part time for your degree while holding down a full-time job, working two or three hours a night and trying the patience of family members as you disappear to study yet again. You've probably pleaded with the boss for more time off, spent lunch times doing research on the Internet and sneaked the odd sickie to get that assignment done. And now you're faced with many free hours and you feel a bit lost. It's nice to have a rest from all that study, but having risen to one challenge, you want another.

If you're still at university, create time *now* to plan your career. This involves participating in activities such as constructive work experience, internships, corporate business games and competitions, networking, voluntary work, attending careers events and research into the job market, considering further study, visiting the careers service in person and online, and analysing your own strengths and capabilities. Allocate even three hours a week out of 168 during your degree and you will be well on the road to securing your immediate future. You'll also have to fill any missing gaps in your CV to strengthen any future job or course applications and make deadlines.

Start building bridges from where you are now to where you want to be. The more foundations you can lay down now, the easier life will be later.

Take control. Get organised

Create a folder – call it something like 'Life After University' – and put everything you need to work on into it. It will save you time searching for pieces of paper and information. If you've got a PC or lap top, create a life and career folder on that, too, for emails and bookmark useful websites you visit regularly.

Then look ahead

There are a number of key decisions you will need to make about your life after your degree. These vary from the urgent and/or important, to those things which simply need to be dealt with, such as, *'What will I do with all my books?'* and *'Which friends do I want to keep in touch with?'* The latter two questions need to be dealt with in order that they don't clutter up your mind and time so that you can focus on the all-important bigger picture.

The urgent decisions are those you need to make today. The important decisions are not usually time pressured but they affect the Big Picture, i.e. your life. An important and urgent decision may be:

do you accept that offer of a post-graduate place you had yesterday? It's Tuesday now; you've got until Thursday at 5 p.m. to decide.

Two major issues which you will almost certainly want to deal with are those of career and finance. Devote more time and energy on the more important issues in life and you'll reap the rewards in the long term. Socialising may be fun but it won't bring you the best rate of return career-wise, nor will it help you pay off any financial debts. Plotting your career and working up the ladder will bring a higher salary, with which you can make positive strides in sorting out your finances and especially your debts.

Let's follow these two areas in life further.

Do career and financial audits

Table 1.1 demonstrates questions to ponder.

Table 1.1

Career	Finance
What do I want to achieve in life?	How much do I owe?
What is important to me?	Who do I owe it to?
What do have I to offer the world?	How much interest am I paying each lender monthly?
What am I going to do next?	
What could I learn to ensure I get to where I want to be?	What could I do to reduce this interest?
What are my ambitions and aspirations, dreams and hopes?	What incomings do I have now?
How far do I want a career which uses the knowledge I've acquired of my subject?	What am I spending it on?
	What do I have left?
	What could I do to cut back on my spending?
Could I go on to further study?	How could I pay back my loans and debts?
Do I need a break?	
Where in the world do I want to work?	Who could help me?
	What could I do to get the best deal on everything?
How far shall I go in my career?	
Where can I get constructive, informed advice (e.g. university careers service, Prospects)?	What could I do to supplement my income?
	When will I start paying everything back?
Who do I need to support me?	Where can I get constructive, informed advice (e.g. bank, building society, student loan company)?
What action(s) will I take to move me closer to where I want to be?	
	What action(s) will I take to achieve my financial and life goals?

Doing an audit like this empowers you because you're choosing to address the situation. You're looking at it head on, dealing with known facts rather than assumptions or guesses. You can move forward by creating an action plan and carrying it out. With regard to debts, it is better to know what your bottom line is in order to prevent yourself getting any further into debt. You may have a student debt of £15,000; but how much further are you prepared to allow yourself to build that up before you start paying it back? £20,000? £30,000? It doesn't mean you'll never go for a wild night out with your friends again but it could mean that you look for other ways to have a wild time so that you can control your finances more tightly. Do it jointly with friends in the same boat. Also, acknowledge that there are times when we don't like the decisions we have to make. They are uncomfortable and don't fit in well with the lifestyle we want. But discipline never did anyone any harm and can frequently bring unexpected rewards, not least of which are self-respect and an in-built self-belief that you can turn an uncomfortable situation around.

Take action now!

1   List the decisions you need to make now and in the next six months.
2   What have you done so far towards making these decisions?
3   What else you need to do or to know in order to decide? How will you get that information and where will you get it from?
4   Whose help will you need?
5   When do you need to make each decision?
6   What action will you take?

Many of the decisions in one area of our life will impact on others. For instance, your career choice will impact on where you live and work, the structure of your life and the people you work with and/or socialise with. It will affect your standard of living and your overall happiness. You may need to undertake further training, learning and development to acquire your professional status. Career choice can determine the hours you work and whether you're on call or not, the pace of your working day and your stress levels. The career you have when you leave university and the effort you put into it will also impact on your ability to pay back your loans and start laying strong financial foundations to your life.

Are you an effective decision maker?

You can learn a lot about yourself from the way you make decisions. Take two decisions you've made about your university life or course. Ask yourself:

1 What motivated you to take these decisions?
2 *How* did you make them? For example, was it by gut instinct, by careful research and thought, weighing up the pros and cons, tossing a coin, following the lead of others, force of circumstance or meeting the expectations of others? What process did you follow?
3 Who influenced your decisions and subsequent actions? Who could you have involved more or less?
4 What, if anything, held you back from making decisions and how did you overcome it?
5 Is a pattern emerging about your decision making? What does it tell you about the way you make decisions? Are there patterns which aren't helping you that you need to change?
6 How can you make your decision making more effective?

In making any decision, there are various factors to take into account as shown in Table 1.2.

Decision-making skills transfer well in life, from making career choices to buying a home. Such skills are essential at work, whether you are self-employed, an employee or the boss, in making business decisions such as the clients you choose to work with, which suppliers you choose to work with and whether you should relocate your business to a more cost-effective area. We can make action plans to implement our decisions but often unexpected obstacles make the journey more of a roller-coaster ride.

Focus on the result you want and the obstacles will shrink

Often, when faced with a decision, we tend to focus too much on possible problems and the negative. *'There are too many graduates...', 'not enough time in the day...', 'I don't want to...'* Prob-

Table 1.2

Possible factors influencing your decision	Choosing modules to study	Choosing your career
Your strengths and skills	What you're naturally good at and wanted to build your skills in	Same for career
Your interests	Following your passions	Same for career – this is what you want to do
What was available?	The modules on offer at your university	What is on offer in the region you work in?
Personal fit	You had a lot of time and respect for the tutor and got on well together; you thought he'd bring out the best in you	You like where the company is going and what it stands for; you met the guys and felt comfortable with them
Long-term plans	You want to go into marketing so this fitted well with your career plans	You choose an employer who can meet your aspirations
How you make decisions	for example '…Ran out of time – just ticked the box for something to do' 'Gut feeling. Everything felt right about this'	for example '…Went for the first thing I saw – can always change later' 'The moment I walked into the place, I knew it was right for me'

lems have a way of shrinking when put into the context of what we really want. Let's say you get the offer of a dream career from an employer you'd love to work for. The only hitch is that you don't know anyone in the town you'd be living in. It's a totally new area to you. *'Where will I live if I go somewhere new?'* you may ask. But compared to the job offer, which you're wild with excitement about, the accommodation problem is minor. You know you'll sort it somehow. You could lodge for a while as you look. Your new colleagues may know about housing opportunities and good inexpensive places to live. The most important thing is that you've done it; you've got the offer you wanted. Housing seems immaterial beside that. You found somewhere to live at university or found time to do your studies while working full time; you can do it again.

Have faith in your own ability to create a life
for yourself even if you move to a place where
you don't know anyone

Yes, it's hard. But you've done it before. Think of all those times
when you've walked into an unknown place and survived. You've
handled it before and now it's time to face it again.

Ten transferable skills you built on at university which will serve
you well in life are the abilities to:

1   start completely afresh – new people, new place, new things to
     learn, new challenges;
2   take part in and contribute to an organisation – previously,
     your university, now the workplace, the community, new
     friends;
3   find your way around and learn the ropes;
4   ask the right questions of the right people to get the answers
     you need;
5   network across the organisation – as important within an em-
     ploying organisation as fun at university;
6   take the initiative and make things happen – a day at univer-
     sity or college which – lectures and tutorials apart – was pretty
     much your own;
7   show how adaptable and flexible you are in juggling work,
     study and social activities, often changing plans at the last
     minute;
8   organise your time;
9   hunt out new friends and like-minded people you can particu-
     larly relate to;
10   relate to people of all different sorts of backgrounds, nation-
     alities and abilities.

University has taught you to think, to question, to be creative, to
challenge, to research, to find solutions to problems and to interact.
Those skills will never be wasted. And the more you stretch yourself
and expand them, the more powerful a resource they will become.

Wait a minute. What's important to you?

Before you start making decisions, consider what's really important
to you. Where are you going? How does the decision fit into the

bigger picture? A key starting point to making successful decisions involves knowing what is right for you in life or work. You need a strong sense of self-worth and self-awareness. These things encompass areas such as the roles you want to play in life: your career interests, ambitions, aspirations, the environments and conditions you thrive in and learn best in, the things you need around you to make you happy and feel fulfilled and those things that are important to you and what you couldn't do without, i.e. your values. Know what you want, and life has more purpose. You'll move faster because you don't deviate from your route spending time doing things you don't want to do. Many people simply wait for that lucky break to knock on their door. Unfortunately, they have a long wait. You can create your own luck, as Dr Wiseman points out in his excellent book *The Luck Factor* (see Further Reading at the end of this book).

When you live by your values, you look forward to the start of a new day or week, and you wake up with a happy heart. Life feels right, you feel fulfilled with a strong sense of your own self-worth. Your goals, hopes and aspirations seem easier to strive for because you're at your best as you work towards them. You know you're making the right choices and decisions and moving in the right direction, and you know what to look for. Similarly, the company which recruits staff with values equal to its own has a good feel about it. The staff are happy, motivated, fulfilled and feel appreciated. They look forward to going to work and are a tight-knit team.

Five signs when life – and work in particular – does not encapsulate your values are:

1   You can't perform properly. You get very tired trying to work at something that doesn't gel with you while pretending that all is well.
2   You're frustrated and short tempered, especially as a new working week looms.
3   It's lonely. Everyone else seems to be on a different wave length to you.
4   You keep thinking, *'There must be more to life than this! What's the point?'* This question persists over time and gets louder in your head, making you increasingly frustrated and more angry.
5   You're disappointed in yourself because you know that you should cut your losses and leave, but you can't find the *courage* to do it.

Of course, you may find the perfect match and then something hinders its progression: a technological innovation, a change in the markets, a drop in demand, restructuring, redundancy. Employers understand that it takes time to find the right match, and when reading your CV, they consider your achievements thus far, your progression, development and future career plans. But you must take responsibility for finding that right career and role. Your CV needs to be presented in such a way that it shows consistency.

Table 1.3 shows examples of life and career values. Which ones are important to you to have or be in your life and career to make you truly happy and feel successful?

Having considered which values are important to you, you can build a life and career which incorporates them. For example, if achievement is very important to you, you could look for careers where results are exceedingly important and measured, such as sales roles. If contribution to society is more important, you could consider the public or voluntary sector.

Select the top eight values which are essential to you from those you've ticked and create a picture of what they mean to you – don't make any assumptions about them. Get the foundations right. If you think that things such as travel, holidays, a good social life and money in the bank are your values, consider what those things *give*

Table 1.3

Winner	Participant	Contributor
Continuous change	Change where needed	Little change
Security	Stability	Risk
Creativity	Performer	Conformity
Compassion	Fair	Faith
Achiever	Influencer	Supporter
Recognition	Status in community	Appreciated
Success	Work–life balance	Fulfilment
Autonomy	Independence	Managed
Visionary	Implement	Support
Adventure	Spirituality	Pleasure
Driver, creator	Follow the leader	Win–win
Wealth	Rewarded	Feel-good factor
Happiness	Freedom	Other

you or *provide you with* and you'll have your real values. Then rank those eight in order. Which one is most important? Which values could you *not* do without? And which are you *not* prepared to compromise on?

Compromising in life will bring more win–wins

At some stage in life, you'll need to compromise. For example, let's say you want to work for an ethical company. However, if the only position you were offered in six months was from a company which was, in your eyes, unethical, what would you do? Would you refuse to take the job and uphold your values or take the offer up and move on as soon as you could?

What happens now?

For many of us, life looks something like Figure 1.1.

In the early years after graduation, most people want to establish themselves by getting a foot on the work and housing ladders.

What about me?

Many graduates have no clear idea of what they want to do after university so the first three to five years often follow the path shown in Figure 1.2.

This runway to the point where your career takes off may be longer and tougher in terms of getting that lucky break, the opportunity or gap in the market, especially as you are probably trying to begin a new life at the same time. You may hook a lower-level job, just to get going. If this is you, you'll need a real rocket thrust of

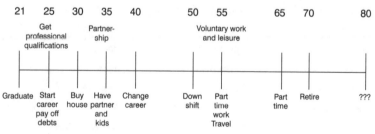

Figure 1.1

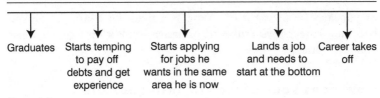

Graduates   Starts temping   Starts applying   Lands a job   Career takes
             to pay off   for jobs he   and needs to   off
             debts and get   wants in the same   start at the bottom
             experience   area he is now

Figure 1.2

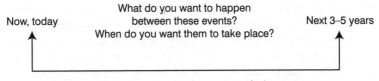

Now, today

What do you want to happen
between these events?
When do you want them to take place?

Next 3–5 years

- Within two years, manage the department of a large store
- More of a strategic role with the company I'm with now
- Have professional qualifications in a business function
- Use my knowledge and expertise to help small companies expand overseas
- Work abroad for two-year assignment
- Have my own business with profitable turnover of £/US$ ...
- Qualified as a ...
- Paid off ...% of my student loans and started to ...
- Settled down into life after university
- Found my partner for life

Figure 1.3

continuous effort to get yourself up to the level you truly aspire to and you need to ask yourself questions about your future, such as those in Figure 1.3. Keep focused on your goal, so that you can be sure you're headed in the right direction. If you lose that focus, your goal will be more difficult to achieve, if indeed it happens at all.

Do you want a job or a career?

Jobs and careers are very different. Jobs fit well into short-term plans and bring the money in, but they don't necessarily stretch you or pay well, which can make you feel bored and disillusioned, especially when you weigh up your salary against your student debts. Careers usually demand professional qualifications and relevant work experience and they involve a ladder which you design and climb rung by rung. You may know what is at the top of this ladder, or you may be taking it one rung at a time. Of course, a job can become a career if you take the initiative, yank it up a gear and get yourself noticed.

How does your career fit into your life?

You need to find the work–life balance that's right for you, something which works for you and your dependants, such as children or elderly parents. At first, this may be hindered as you devote time to establishing yourself and getting a foot on the work and housing ladders, putting bricks and blocks down to get the life you want – the house, family life, network of friends, security, professional qualifications where appropriate, the opportunity for advancement and professional growth, recognition and appreciation. Of course, you may prefer to focus on having fun, rather than sorting out your career and life. *Well, there's always next year.*

A hunger for success at work can seriously impact on your quality of life. If your goal was to make your first million within three years after leaving university, and you succeeded but you lost all your friends in the process because you were always working, would you still deem that a success? Some graduate programmes demand that you dedicate 60, 70, 80 or even 90 per cent of your life to work. You may be prepared to give that early in your career if it takes you to where you really want to be, or you may prefer to opt for a more sensible work–life balance which takes you to a rung on the ladder which you're happy with.

What matters is the *degree of control* we each have over our work–life balance. If you decide to work 100 hours a week to make that first million, that's your choice. Work–life balance becomes an issue when we feel we *don't* have a choice; that other people are making decisions for us about the hours we need to put in. Some employers place a higher priority on work–life balance than others. The most demanding employer may be the person who runs their own business.

As you create a vision of your future career, build specifics into the picture so that you can build plans around them in response to the questions in Figure 1.3 on page 11. For example:

- What is your career goal, outcome or end result? If it makes things easier, look at this over a three- to five-year period.
- Why is this important to you?

- How exactly is your career important to you?
- Where do you want to be doing it in the next three to five years?
- When are your timescales/deadlines for achieving your goal?
- Who will you be doing it with?
- Who can help you?
- How will you get there? What are the different ways you could reach the outcome you want?
- What can you do to boost your chances of success?
- What can you control? What is outside your control?
- Which deadlines do you need to look out for, such as applying for post-graduate courses, work experience placements and internships?
- What in life and in your career are you not prepared to risk, e.g. your integrity, values, standards, expectations of yourself, key relationships; and what are you prepared to risk?

The *why* is important. If you don't understand *why* something is important to you, it is far less likely to happen. If you can see how a goal relates to your values – for example keeping fit is important to you because you value good health – then you're more likely to achieve it.

Wherever you are, pinpoint careers help available to you

Find out what careers advisory services are available to you where you are *now*, face-to-face, online and by telephone. Sometimes you just need to sit down and talk through your future with someone whom you can trust and who is impartial. Any careers adviser or coach should be qualified and trained. Tap into local universities and colleges, your old university and other private agencies in your area for access to careers information, as well as using the Internet. Most higher education institutions allow graduates to use their facilities for up to two or three years after graduation and will also help graduates from any university wishing to move into, remain in or return to their area. You may be charged for some services. See Useful Addresses at the end of this book for details.

Finally, don't forget that your degree has taught you many transferable skills. Use the forward and strategic planning skills you acquired throughout your degree experience to plan your career. Take the initiative and put your brain and energy to work.

Summary action points

Look back at your life overall:

1   How much has it consisted of what you want so far? What efforts have you put in to make sure that happened?
2   What clues do your past choices give you as you look to your future?
3   What do you want to achieve *in your life* in the next five years? What would that mean to you?

Chapter 2

Creating your career

This chapter is all about helping you to create a vision of what you want your career to consist of. Even if you already have a picture, use the self-assessment exercises to add depth to it. Stand back and look at yourself, as if you were looking at the ground from a helicopter, and the distance will help you think more clearly.

Ten questions to consider

1 What are my passions and motivators?
2 How far do I want to climb the career ladder and what career goals, outcome or end result do I want?
3 What do I want to achieve?
4 What skills and knowledge do I want to use and how do I want to use my degree knowledge and skills?
5 What do I want to achieve and consequently contribute to an organisation's mission?
6 What role do I want to have?
7 Which specific products or areas of expertise do I want to work with?
8 Who do I want to work for and what sort of clients and customers do I want to work for?
9 What sort of working environment do I want to work in?
10 What's of key importance to me in my career?

Let's consider some of these in greater detail.

Before you start, list the core and optional modules and courses you studied at university. Include projects and assignments you undertook and work experience you had. Keep them in mind as you work through the questions which arise in this chapter.

What are your passions and motivators?

If you want to be happy and successful in your career, get passionate. Find something to do which really inspires and motivates you and stirs you to action, which gives you a real buzz. This is all about your vocation and reason for working.

- What excites you and inspires you?
- What are you passionate about?
- What makes you angry? What do you want to make a difference to?
- What do you want to particularly do something about?
- How do you want to make a difference to the world?
- What secret dreams and aspirations do you have?
- What makes you jump out of bed in the morning?

How far do you want to climb up the career ladder?

Do you want to work at the professional, senior manager and associate professional levels or are you more in tune with those of administrative, secretarial and personal service? Of course, you can move from the latter group up into the former. If you start out your graduate career in administration, you can move into the higher level category, provided that you focus on where you are going. Some administrative roles in the public and education sectors are graduate positions from the outset. Equally, you may want to start your own company or social enterprise.

What does career success look like to you? As you climb the career ladder, where are you and what are you doing when you reach your top rung? When do you want to get there? Examples of responsibilities at the top of a career ladder or close to it include:

1   Management responsibilities, perhaps for a region with a number of branches, or one large department store or factory.
2   Joint or solo responsibility for the strategic direction the organisation takes.
3   High local profile in the community.
4   Doing something rewarding for society, the community, the world.
5   Running your own company, be it online or on the ground, in the street.

6   Advising companies on solving problems – where they call you in.

7   The financial rewards … money, profit, lifestyle to match.

8   Being on a company's Board of Directors.

9   Ensuring smooth running of a business, possibly behind the scenes.

10 Having fun at work – you enjoy getting up in the morning and heading to the office.

Once you've reached one stage (for example, a Regional Manager) and become fully effective in it, you may look long term to the next goal (for example, becoming a Director in the company), and so you work your way up the rungs of the ladder, either having a long-term view from the start or making your way up step by step. The skills you need change as you move up. Leadership and management skills of others and yourself become even more important as you take on responsibility for others. Strategic thinking, forward planning and risk taking will also feature highly as you rise to the top of a company. If you're self-employed, you will need to use these skills rigorously so that you know where your own company and efforts are going.

Does your idea of career success incorporate professional qualifications?

If your answer is 'yes, it does', be prepared to devote extra hours after a long day's work to study and train, attend courses, sit examinations, undertake projects and do research. You may need to commit two or three nights a week to study, plus most weekends. With good time management, discipline and focus, you can do it, just as many students have done before you. Once achieved, professional qualifications cannot be taken away from you. And they open doors. Many FTSE 100 companies have professionally qualified people on their Boards. But, as in any game, you'll need a strategy to win.

What skills do you want to use in your career?

A Business Studies degree (including Administration, Finance, Accountancy and International Business) opens the door to many careers, especially if you have language skills. The question is: what are the key skills you've developed through the course and how far do you want to apply all or any one or two of them to your role at work, i.e. your career?

Skills your degree will have taught you when working on your own or with a group, include, in particular:

1   decision making using quantitative and qualitative skills;
2   identifying and solving business problems;
3   evaluating arguments and evidence in a critical way;
4   creating, evaluating, assessing and deciding on a range of options;
5   applying business ideas and knowledge to various situations;
6   communicating using a range of methods, all of which can be used at work;
7   researching, preparing and presenting business reports;
8   locating, extracting and analysing data and making recommendations from your findings;
9   using ICT (information and communications technology) in the workplace;
10 the ability to learn, and to manage your own career;
11 researching business and management problems and issues using relevant and appropriate primary and secondary tools, research sources;
12 critical thinking, such as identifying assumptions and generalisations, looking for evidence and detecting false logic or reasoning.

In addition, you can see the big picture, yet pay attention to detail. You can come up with an idea, persuade other people of its benefits, and put plans into action to make it happen. Many of these skills are transferable, such as communicating, i.e. you can transfer them from one job to another. The vast majority of careers need such skills, some to a higher degree of competence than others, depending on the level you are at. But careers also require their own specific job-related skills which will impact on the activities you do all day. For example, a buyer may select and price goods, develop a close relationship with suppliers, arrange for their distribution, plan a range of products, decide what products should be promoted and when and research the market. A financial adviser advises, informs, possibly promotes and recommends products, assesses a client's needs, guides them to the right choice and helps them complete any necessary documentation. Table 2.1 gives examples of transferable and job-specific skills.

Using the above list as a guide, consider the following questions.

1 Which skills have you developed or practised through your university life and academic studies? Build a picture around them. For example, you can apply IT, ideas, knowledge and concepts.
2 Which would apply to any graduate of any discipline? (These are the transferable skills.)

Table 2.1

Achieving	Evaluating	Presenting
Acquiring	Finding solutions	Pricing
Administering	Fundraising	Problem solving
Advising	Guiding	Processing
Analysing	Helping	Producing
Answering	Identifying	Programming
Applying	Implementing	Project management
Assembling	Influencing	Promoting
Assessing	Innovating	Qualitative skills
Building	Inspiring	Quantitative skills
Buying	Interviewing	Questioning
Caring	Inventing	Recommending
Challenging	Investigating	Researching
Classifying	Keeping records	Securing
Coaching	Learning	Selecting
Cold calling	Liaising	Selling
Communicating	Listening	Servicing
Conducting	Locating	Setting targets
Conserving	Making	Studying
Consulting	Managing	Summarising
Counselling	Marketing	Supervising
Creating	Mentoring	Supporting
Critical thinking	Monitoring	Taking risks
Dealing	Motivating	Talking
Debating	Negotiating	Teaching
Designing	Networking	Teamworking
Detecting, e.g. false	Numeracy	Training
logic	Operating	Understanding
Developing	Organising	Watching
Diagnosing	Persuading	Winning
Displaying	Planning	Writing
Distributing	Preparing	Other

3   Look back to achievements that you're really proud of. Which skills did you excel at and which did you enjoy using? Often we use these skills in informal situations, such as counselling a friend; but we also use them in more formal settings, such as promoting a concert or teaching English. Which might relate to work settings?

4   Which skills do you want to use at work in the future? Do you need to learn them from scratch or build on those you already have?

5   Which roles at work or careers need these skills?

The last question is the trickier one because you need a basic overview of the careers market to start identifying potential roles. A programme such as Prospects Planner (visit www.prospects.ac.uk to find out more) may help you make the link between your skills and possible good career matches. But think about those careers and organisations where the skills you've identified are needed. For example, if you would like to communicate over the telephone frequently, a career in headhunting or sales may suit, as you need to do a lot of cold calling.

If you've identified the skill of researching, what exactly do you want to research? If dealing with people appeals to you, a career as a head-hunter or researcher could be right for you. This involves researching and identifying possible candidates for a role your company has been asked to fill, and then cold calling them to try to assess their suitability and interest. Later, you would interview potential candidates, usually senior managers and executives, and help negotiate a final offer for the successful candidate. The ability to manage clients and build effective working relationships would be important. Your clients would expect you to have a strong network of possible candidates and a thorough knowledge of the sector you specialise in, including salary trends.

You could also consider working for recruitment consultants, who tend to deal with lower levels of staff than head-hunters and more likely to work on a regional or local patch. There are more of these throughout a country because there are more positions to fill at the lower levels. If you work for a national or regional recruitment agency and progress, you may have responsibility for a team of consultants, thereby enjoying a management and leadership role.

What about knowledge?

You have acquired knowledge specific to your studies on areas such as markets, customer expectations and service standards, finance, managing and developing people, operations and finance, and information and communications technology; business policy and strategy, developing appropriate policies and strategies in a changing environment to meet a goal or mission; and issues relating to the current business environment, such as innovation, creativity, enterprise, knowledge economy and management, sustainability, diversity, ethics, and globalisation. Creativity is particularly important to businesses as they search for the smartest ways to do things and motivate their staff, and to innovate new products and services their customers want. Design plays a key role in ensuring that businesses can function as effectively as possible and that a building enhances employees' motivation to work and perform.

You may have acquired a very high level of knowledge already in a particular subject, such as accountancy, either by focusing entirely on it in your degree studies or choosing options within a broader degree which gave you the opportunity to build your knowledge. It may have already given you insight into the terminology, rules and practices of the subject, plus a clear insight into the contexts in which it operates, such as the public sector, charities or the profession itself. This may be specific to the country where you did your degree studies. The skills you will have acquired as a result of your degree will never be wasted. The question is, do you deepen your knowledge and status further, perhaps by taking professional qualifications or a graduate trainee programme, or pursue a generalist approach whereby you work at a number of different business functions, or change career altogether?

What role do you want to have?

Look at this question now, then fast forward in your mind to six months' time, a year's time and three to five years' time. People play different roles within a team and a company, often at once. If you're self-employed, you may be company owner, manager, doing the work and fulfilling your vision all at once. A Finance Director who has overall responsibility for finance will probably have management responsibilities of a department if he works in a medium–large sized company, as he will lead a team.

Think about the roles you've played in your life in all the teams you've participated in. Are you a natural leader or do you prefer to be a supportive player? If, within a team, you prefer to support a leader, then running your own business may not be for you. Which roles do you want to become adept at and what sort of training and experiences would you need to make this happen? Each of the roles below contribute to the overall business, but in different ways. Which one(s) appeal to you? In part, that will depend on the results you want to achieve (see page 24). Table 2.2 gives examples of a number of roles.

Weigh up the pros and cons of each role and consider them in light of your life and career values. If achievement is important to you in your values, then being a leader, manager or entrepreneur in sales may appeal. Each role calls for different qualities and values, but they all operate in a wide range of sectors and fields.

An exciting role which can be very much what you make of it is that of support. An example is an Executive Assistant or Personal Assistant, supporting and working closely with senior management. Many at this level enjoy considerable influence, determining who should have access to their boss and when, delegating much of his or her work to other senior managers, liaising with the Board including captains of industry, and having control of budgets, sometimes in their millions. Many entrepreneurs want sharp, commercially oriented graduate calibre and frequently bi-lingual PAs or EAs, capa-

Table 2.2

Leader the boss team leader	*Technician* doing the technical aspects as opposed to strategic and business planning
Team player working with a group of people to achieve a particular goal or mission	*Back office* administration, ensuring things run smoothly, e.g. office support, office manager, PA, operations
Employee bank, building society	*Entrepreneur* creating a business out of a vision
Manager project manager implementing vision	*Freelance support* providing a service or product to businesses as and when required
Company owner e.g. small business owner	*Front line* client-relationship managers bankers

ble of delegating, organising, managing, networking, researching, analysing and presenting arguments. The responsibilities you take depends on the sector you join; the PA working for a hedge fund company, for example, may spend some of their day tracking funds and liaising with clients, whereas a PA in a PR company may spend a lot of time organising events and liaising with the media. Indeed, the PA role can be a great place to launch your career from and gain insight into and experience of a (large) company, provided that you have clearly defined goals and work to make them happen. You can also learn a great deal from the boss – and then set off to run your own company, perhaps providing services to companies as a virtual assistant.

Another role is that of the Office Manager, who has responsibility for all facets of running an office, including tasks such as managing the building, supervising support staff, handling health and safety aspects and running a budget. Such a role involves strong organising and influencing skills, with a degree of strategic planning and lots of initiative. This could involve finding new premises and supervising an office move.

Many support roles involve a degree of supervising staff, distributing work load, recruiting and training new staff, assessing and appraising team members, promoting a team environment and co-ordinating team meetings. There are also roles involving space and head count, management reporting, creating presentations and doing the necessary research and delegating. In many organisations, executive and personal assistants and office managers need to have strong interpersonal skills and confidence to influence, negotiate and communicate their plans for the smooth running of the office.

What do you want to achieve and consequently contribute to an organisation's mission?

What sort of results and achievements really turn you on and give you a good *'I've got to achieve this!'* feeling? How can these results contribute to an organisation and where would you need to be placed to achieve them? What contribution do you want to make? Consider potential employers, what sort of missions should they be on that you want to be a part of? It could be helping companies grow by offering them business advice and support as a consultant. Perhaps it's making the company the number one customer choice

Table 2.3

Clinching the deal	Exceeding targets
Highest takings	Influencing individuals
Greatest number of arrests	New policy/procedure
A profit	Recognition (from whom?)
Influencing groups	Justice
Strong motivated team	Highest number of commissions
Idea going into fruition	A new approach
Influencing the direction of some-	Happy customers
thing	Famous for what I do
A new look	Huge profits
Recommendations put in effect	Group effort
Take-over of a company	Building relationships/businesses
A sale	Making a difference to a country
Money	Making a difference to the world
Helping an individual	Seeing your ideas in action
Making an immediate impact	Other

in the sector, or giving young people inspiration and hope. What results do you want to achieve as part of a team? Table 2.3 gives examples of results.

How hungry are you to make these results happen?

Look at the results you've highlighted. Are you ravenous to take them on board, or just wanting to nibble at them? How fulfilled would you be if you achieved your results every working day, 48 weeks of the year? You need that hunger and passion to make an impact and get the results you want. If you nibble at something, it will be less fulfilling. Look for a cause, a passion, interest or aspiration you really are ready to tackle. Compare it to your favourite meal your mother's cooked for you when you get home on that first night from university at the end of term. Aim to feel that hunger every time you start working for the result you want. Look for something which really hits the spot.

What does the picture of success look like to you?

Do you see a healthy bank account, flashy car, exotic holidays and so on? Or is it more about leaving the office having done something great for the good of society or a charity that day; the feel-good factor is more important than pay and a wealthy lifestyle.

Examples

Richard is very ambitious, focused and driven by money. He has had many sales jobs in his career, with lots of experience in selling acquired through a range of holiday and Saturday jobs, and also working in a call centre for a bank. He wants to get to the top as quickly as he can and get well rewarded for his efforts. He is passionate about property and wants to get a position in a company where he can work as a lettings agent or estate agent, preferably the former. He envisages a career where he can build up a team and take responsibility for a number of offices in a national company. His business degree included studies in strategic management and developing and motivating people, which will enable him to take a long-term view of his career and the role he takes on. He is planning to do an MBA in two years' time after acquiring some experience at work.

Suki took a business studies degree too, but, while ambitious – she wants to be a partner with a firm of accountants within ten years – she is driven by the thought of obtaining her professional qualifications and finding her niche working for a small to medium-sized firm of accountants in her local area. She has good numerical skills, but a project in her business degree proved to her that she had good business skills. She wants to stay in her local area and make a name for herself among small business owners, particularly women.

What sector do you want to work in?

What sparks your interest and intrigues you hour after hour? Projects you chose to work on could provide you with hints as to which sector you would like to work in. Some roles and careers are required in every sector; for example, you could be an accountant for an airline, engineering company, hotel group or charity. Your choice of sector makes a difference, your performance will be enhanced if you believe in what the company stands for and if you're passionate about the work it does. Table 2.4 shows how the careers classification index (CRCI) breaks down occupations into sectors.

Within each sector, there are many specialist and niche areas, many of which are run by small companies throughout a country as opposed to being in one or two geographic locations. For instance, Table 2.5 shows that the financial/business services sector covers many areas.

Table 2.4

Administration, Business and Office Work	Leisure, Sport and Tourism
Building and Construction	Manufacturing and Production
Catering and Hospitality	Marketing and Advertising
Computers and IT	Media, Print and Publishing
Design, Art and Crafts	Performing Arts
Education and Training	Personal and Cleaning Support Services
Engineering	Retail Sales and Customer Services
Environment, Animals and Plants	Science, Mathematics and Statistics
Financial Services	Security and Armed Forces
Healthcare	Social Work and Counselling Services
Languages, Information and Culture	Transport and Logistics
Legal and Political Services	

Again, these break down into more niche areas. E-commerce covers business to business, business to customer and customer to customer. Each will be very different forms of business selling different products and services. There's nothing to stop you setting up your own online company or do you want to work for an existing one?

Think about what you want to achieve in work and what interests you. If you're heading into HR, you need to be able to understand employment law and how it relates to working practices and organisations. In a large company, you could move into a business function niche. Within HR, for example, many large corporates have specialist employees in Employee Benefits and Compensation; Recruitment; Training and Development. The HR arena also is a first-class example of the classic role which is misunderstood. It is as much

Table 2.5

Compensation claims	Debt advice and counselling
Insurance	Banks
Accountants	Building societies
Book-keepers	Cheque cashing
Actuaries	Credit and finance companies
Life assurance and pensions	Ecommerce
Payroll services	Finance brokers
Secretarial/Virtual assistant services	Financial advisers
Call centres	Mortgages
Internet services	Venture capitalists
Export finance	Business consultants
Bankruptcy	Bureau de change
Insolvency practitioners	Business valuers
Debt Collecting agencies	Business enterprise agencies
Investment and trust companies	

about developing people and ensuring that the organisation has the right mix of skills, qualities, experience and motivated staff to meet business goals going forward as it is about hiring and firing.

Some may not be the sexy front-line roles that many graduates crave, yet businesses cannot function without them and, in recent years, changes in technology and the structure of organisations have made them far more suitable for graduates. It all goes back to the role we want to play at work. Those who succeed in them will be those people with the ability to influence and negotiate with others, to make their point (remember those times you've put forward your case in tutorials and made your point in presentations) and have a bit of get-up-and-go about them. We're not talking about data entry and pushing buttons here but collecting data, analysing it and making recommendations, often across departments. Additionally, many organisations will take on project managers who can implement various programmes of any nature and who have strong IT skills. Compliance and company secretarial roles also demand a strong degree of self-confidence and persuasive and influencing skills to ensure the organisation keeps to the right side of the law and industry regulations.

Taking another different sector as an example, marketing is a very popular career choice for graduates, and a business studies degree will prepare you well for it. But there are a huge range of career options within it. Figure 2.1 shows just a few of them.

Are there specific products or areas of expertise you want to work with?

Managing means taking control of, to be in charge of, or to handle. In the workplace, you can become a specialist manager, such as a Finance Manager or Human Resource Manager, or you can be a generalist manager. Consider the options in Table 2.6

Whatever your management responsibilities cover, be it people, money, sales or anything else, you will be expected to perform, so that your efforts impact on the bottom line, staff motivation and customers' satisfaction. Your efforts can be held against a benchmark that is measured in percentages, figures, profit margins, the number of complaints and meeting of deadlines. In short, your effectiveness and drive for achievement can truly be measured.

Many graduate programmes in the larger companies give you the ability to work in a number of these, six months in each department,

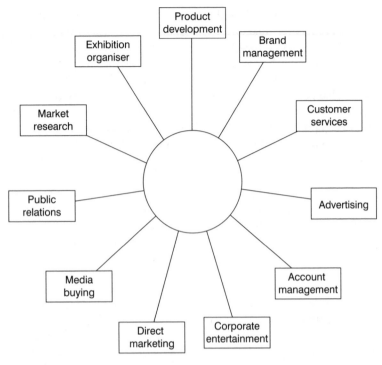

Figure 2.1

so that you can see where your skills and qualities are best suited and acquire an understanding of how all the various sections link together. But you don't have to get 'in' in this way. You'll almost certainly need work experience, to prove that you know what the work involves, so why not approach a company and ask if you can shadow someone there for a few days to give you insight? If you like what you see, you can get their advice on what to do next and the best ways 'in'. You could consider getting a temporary position in, for example, an HR department, start picking up the right experience and then go from there to find a position, studying for your professional examinations part-time. They won't necessarily recruit you for your degree, but for your willingness to learn and to manage your own career development and hunger for progression.

In a small company, you'll probably acquire a lot of knowledge about many areas, whereas in a large company, you're more likely to become an expert in one very focused field. In smaller companies, one person may have responsibility for a number of areas, while in

Table 2.6

Money, budgets General management Finance Accountancy Banks, building societies Financial advisers	*Laws/regulations* Health and safety Compliance Company secretary Human Resources
People Training and Development Human Resources Recruitment Teaching Lecturing Training/coaching	*Ideas* Product development Design and creativity Advertising Business development Innovation Enterprise
Targets Recruitment Sales Customer service	*Products* Marketing Product development Distributing Buyer
Processes Product development Disaster management Distribution manager	*Systems* IT Disaster management
Events/Conferences/Exhibitions Selling Organising Advertising	*Risk* Actuaries Traders Risk management Insurance
Services Marketing Customer service Insurance	*Buildings* Facilities management Health and safety Operations management

the larger ones, there may be very specific areas and people dealing with one issue on its own, such as facilities management. There may be an overlap between the areas outlined above or they may stand alone. Post-holders may be asked to take on extra areas of responsibility as they arise, which is why a flexible, enthusiastic approach is so important. A facilities manager and office manager may be one and the same person and have responsibility for disaster management. In one respect, this is no bad thing: it widens your experience of working in organisations and companies and may land you in an area where you know you belong and that it definitely is the right place to be. You are unlikely to find specialists in small companies.

You could set up a business offering services to small companies in HR, IT, Marketing etc. as a consultant or freelance. The bigger companies will have their HR, Marketing, PR etc. departments which will, in global organisations, work to implement global policies while taking local niceties and laws and regulations into account.

What sort of clients and customers do you want to work for?

Who do you want your clients and customers to be? How much of your day do you want to spend with external clients and how much do you want to spend looking after those who work for the firm?

If, for example, you're keen to look after the internal needs of a company, you could consider roles such as company secretary, HR, IT, office manager, EA or PA and finance. Many of these roles will still involve liaising with clients (an EA or PA may have a strong client focus role, for example) but others will be far less so. On the other hand, someone working in a PR, financial advisory or accountancy role will have far more to do with external clients. Some companies, such as PR, may focus on specific industries such as food and drink, so it helps to have an interest in those sectors so that you can keep up to date with trends and developments. Much will depend on the industry in the area. If you have an accountant's practice in rural and coastal England, they will probably have considerable expertise in advising the farming and fishing communities. Many recruitment agencies specialise in a specific sector, such as education, media, finance and charities. Their clients all come from specific sectors and you'll build up a very thorough knowledge of those areas. So consider who you want your clients and customers to be and the products you want to work with. The retail market is very diverse, for example, with a huge choice ranging from toy companies such as Toys 'R Us to wine with companies such as Majestic.

Who do you want your colleagues to be and what sort of people do you want them to be like? Also, who do you care passionately about and would do anything for? The following are examples of groups you could work with. In each case, imagine what it would be like working with each group from 9 to 5 every working day. Talk to people who do work in these scenarios. Find out the pros and cons. Build up a picture of what it would be like to work with them, day in and day out. Pinpoint those you would most like to work with in Table 2.7

Table 2.7

Professionals	People with problems
Business-to-business	Different nationalities
Consumers, personal	Under 18s
The general public	All ages
Public sector	Other
Politicians	

Who do you want to work for?

This can make a huge difference to the ethos of the organisation, be it private, public or voluntary sector. It can affect your pay, long-term working conditions and the sort of work you do. Some offer the promise of a better work–life balance; public and voluntary organisations tend to be better at this than the private sector. Examples are shown in Table 2.8.

Talk to people in different companies to find out what life is like and compare notes of those you speak to.

What sort of working environment do you want to work in?

This covers a number of areas. Do you want to work for an organisation where the pace is fast and frenzied with constant deadlines, or do you prefer something a little more sedate? Also, how far do you want to enjoy an international perspective in your career? Consider how much travelling you want to do in your career:

♦ Working in another country with an occasional visit home?
♦ Travelling all the time, e.g. sales rep continually on the road?
♦ Working with people of different cultures and customs?
♦ Travelling frequently as part of your job within your home country?

Table 2.8

Community	Dot.com
Government	Micro-business (under 5)
Private sector	Small businesses (5–49)
Charity	Medium-sized business (50–250)
International organisation	Large business (250–499)
Yourself	Corporate (500+)
Social enterprise	

+ Working abroad for a couple of years in one office?
+ Being the only person from your country while working abroad?
+ Picking up work as you travel – blow your career?
+ Helping international businesses grow?

There is a huge difference working for an international organisation as opposed to a domestic one. Once you've experienced the former, it can be very hard to go back to the latter. In an international career, you'll be working with people from all over the world on the phone, in face-to-face meetings, video conferences, by email and letter. You may need to take conference calls at 4 a.m. to fit in with other time zones. Global companies will have worldwide systems and procedures to follow which may be tiresome at times and will certainly affect the company's culture.

Many medium-sized companies are located in one region with branches throughout it, serving the local community or companies moving to the area. This may give you the opportunity to experience life in different offices, and even rise through the ranks faster than if you were working for a large organisation.

Building on your research skills

Do you want to further your knowledge and research skills? There are currently over 20,000 people engaged in research in the UK. Many work on a project full time, or combine research with other responsibilities such as lecturing or clinical practice, often with others in the UK or abroad. Researchers are often also employed by research councils, the government, and other relevant organisations to fulfil various responsibilities such as management, policy advice and project planning. As well as considering the usual academic routes, find out what bodies such as Regional Development Agencies (www.englandsrdas.com) are doing in your sector to support the movement of knowledge and ideas out of their scholarly world into industry and commerce. There may be funding to enhance these efforts. These agencies may be targeting specific industries or 'cluster groups' which they see as having particularly strong potential for economic growth in their region.

The Research Assessment exercise means that the higher education funding bodies can distribute funds for research on quality. Find out more by visiting www.rae.ac.uk for information on the Research

Assessment Exercise 2008; and www.hero.ac.uk/rae for the 2001 results. Ratings range from 1 to 5* and it gives an idea of the standard of UK research. See Further Reading and Useful Addresses at the end of this book. The normal route into research is to undertake a post-graduate course (Chapter 3 has more information).

What would be of key importance to you in your future career?

Regardless of the careers you may have in mind, identify the elements of work which are key to you in your future such as are shown in Table 2.9.

Moving your self-awareness forward

Your next step is to find out as much as you can about each industry to uncover the real range of employment opportunities within it. Look at the pros and cons – every industry has them – you need to know what you're letting yourself in for. The sector's professional body or trade association will be a good place to start. Chapter 4 will outline how such an organisation can help. Sites such as Prospects, Hobson and AGCAS have sector profiles, country profiles, and more to help you, written for graduates.

Once you have started to work out where you want to be and what you want to be doing, create your own goal or desired result – whatever you choose to call it. You're far more likely to achieve what you want if it is personal to you, reflects your values and it excites you. Create a clear picture of what life will be like when you achieve your goal. Write your goal down as specifically as you can,

Table 2.9

Motivation	Results/outcomes
Purpose of work	Independence
Location	Entrepreneurship
Contribution to organisation/world/ sector/individuals	Personal fit – feeling that you belong? Skills you use
Sector – matching interests and knowledge	Values, as you identified in Chapter 1 Fit with lifestyle
Rules, ethics and behaviour	Knowledge you use
Role	Creativity
Rewards	Fun
Work for me rather than anyone else	

to help you focus, and put it somewhere you can see it every day. Talk about what you do want to do – as opposed to what you don't – as if it were already happening. Give it a time limit, so that you have something to work for. Finally, make it sufficiently challenging to stretch you, but realistic. It will be more manageable if you break it down into bits, so that you can work out step-by-step what needs to be done and when.

An example of a long-term career goal is:

In three years' time, I will have:

> ➢ qualified as an independent financial adviser;
> ➢ paid off 40 per cent of my student debt;
> ➢ a network of friends in London I feel I know really well.

In six months' time, I will have:

> ➢ researched all the firms I want to apply to;
> ➢ found out what I need to do to qualify;
> ➢ made the necessary networking contacts;
> ➢ attended my first job interview.

Ask the right high quality questions and you're more likely to get high quality answers

---

Summary action points

Bringing all the answers to the exercises in this chapter together:

1   What sort of a picture of my future career is emerging? What am I doing in it?
2   What information do I need to firm this picture up?
3   What do I need to happen next to help me further my career plans?
4   What do I need to know to start making decisions?

Chapter 3

Next steps to achieving your goals

As you start building a picture of your future career and life, consider what you need to do to position yourself to make it all happen. Create an action plan, incorporating elements such as constructive work experience, networking, lots of CV writing, possibly more study. The next five chapters will cover these ingredients. There is also the issue of where you want to live and how you will fund your next steps.

This chapter seeks to give you a brief introduction to some of the opportunities you could consider after your degree. Which ones would be most suitable as a stepping stone to the career you want?

What could your next steps be?

Imagine filming yourself on video at work immediately after university. Then wind the film forward to three or to five years' time. Where are you and what are you doing? Your answers will help you plot your path to success by breaking the longer period down into manageable chunks and tackle them one by one. It's then easier to focus on where you're headed.

Your next steps could involve all or any of the following, as shown in Figure 3.1.

Depending on your career and life plans, one may be more appropriate for you than the others. They may all feature at some time in your working life, either alone or in combination and you may not even plan for them. They may just appear as an opportunity too good to miss. You may feel like a complete break from academia and work, and decide to take six months out. But even if you get some work first to help fund it, don't just plump for anything. Try to find something which fulfils your interests and which will help you lay the foundations for your future career.

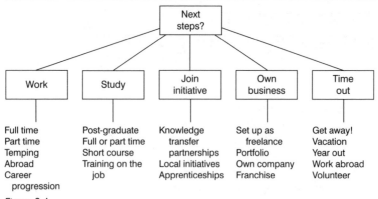

Figure 3.1

What are your employment options?

Graduates have a wider choice of careers than ever before. This choice has been increasing in length and breadth over the decades, moving from a range of careers for which a degree was essential, such as teachers, medical sciences and veterinary science, to those areas where, increasingly, employers sought graduates as their first choice. Initially, this occurred in areas such as management, administrative posts in the public and private sector, but recently degrees have been sought by new sectors. Examples include management accountancy, sales and marketing and buying and purchasing. Many of these now have graduate trainee schemes.

There are also, increasingly, the back office support roles in operations and compliance, administration and office management. This is especially so as executive assistants and personal assistants increasingly take on the work of junior and middle management. Many micro-businesses and one-man bands (such as politicians and entrepreneurs) want to take on graduates as personal assistants or executive assistants because they know they will take the initiative, be able to write speeches and draw up presentations, do the research and make recommendations.

In these areas where graduates are fairly new, you will need to be particularly pro-active in ensuring that your career develops in the way that you want it to. Chapters 6 and 9 go into this in more detail because there are a number of things you can do to help yourself. Entry into many of these areas is being smoothed over through initiatives created by government agencies, such as the Knowledge

Transfer Partnerships, and structured internships and work experience placements. Check to see what your region is doing to help you make an entry.

There are also many graduates moving into areas for which a degree is not required which fall into the 'assistant' role. A large number of graduates go into retail, bar and restaurant work, and lower-level administrative roles. Graduates tend to take on such roles more to start work than anything else, or perhaps to save money to go travelling. It is these roles which, if you choose to take them, will be harder to pull yourself out of and it is these roles which won't pay the salaries and perks usually enjoyed by so many graduates elsewhere. It is at this level that dissatisfaction may rise to give thoughts such as *'Why did I go to university and land myself with such a debt?'* You may also find that you miss out on other company activities which other graduates enjoy, such as a development programme or course. Strategic planning can help you work your way out of it. You will need to assess, plot and plan, monitor and review your progress.

Enrolling for professional qualifications

You may plan to study for professional qualifications once you have decided on the business function you wish to work with. These give you the core knowledge and competences which you need to perform effectively at work; they give you the theory and practice which gives you a competitive edge. In some industries, you cannot advise clients or practice without them. Working towards them normally involves both practical experience and sitting a number of exams. Consider which is best for you (talk about this with your employer, but do some fact finding about professional qualifications as you move through your career decision-making process). Think about how you want to study, be it online, by evening class, through block learning or distance learning. Professional bodies will have a list of accredited training providers and most have a very considerable range of support mechanisms to help you through.

Temping ... the perfect way in, or a mug's game?

Many graduates temp to give themselves time to decide what they want to do. It's a great way to find the right role. Company and temp can try each other out to ensure they are a good match in terms of personality, aspirations and skill-set. As a temp, when that permanent offer comes, it can be hard to give up the flexibility of temping, but it is good not to have to worry about those times when there is no work available. You'll never know whether you have a job from one week to the next, so enrol with more than one agency because when times get tough, temps can be the first people to be let go.

Temping is not an easy ride. You're not just representing yourself and the employer you're working for, but the agency which placed you there. The more IT packages you can offer and the more flexible you are in terms of where you work, the more likely you will be to secure work. Remember that networking and showing what you can do and telling people what you want to do will play a key role in landing that all-important first post.

Agencies are businesses seeking to make a profit, so take responsibility for plotting and planning your own career. Above all, keep your eye on your career and the goal you're heading for. The danger of temping is that you could still find yourself temping after a year, with no further progress in your decision making, so enlist the help of a mentor – perhaps someone you get on with well at work or someone you find via a professional organisation – to help you stay on track. Even temporary posts can form an important part of your career planning, which gives you a fresh approach to the roles you're taking on rather than simply saying, 'Oh it pays the bills...' When you're deciding which agencies to sign up with, look at their websites and track record. Who are their main clients? Do they appeal to you? Make the experience a constructive one. If you can take on a project, even voluntarily, for a company to help boost your CV and skill set, then make the most of the opportunity to be in the right place at the right time.

Temping is a great way to boost your ability to handle change, as you cope regularly with new assignments and, consequently, changes in dress code, the standards of behaviour expected, new colleagues, office software and journeys to work. You may think you feel you're being treated like an imbecile. Do your mode of dress and behaviour make you look like one? Even if you're simply photocopying something, people can tell a lot about you from the way you approach the task. The next placement could prove to demand every brain cell you've got, so take the rough with the smooth.

Studied part-time while working?

Look back at the reasons why you enrolled for a degree, under-graduate or post-graduate. Perhaps you did so with your employer's knowledge, blessing and support. If this is the case, discuss your future with your employer, your direct boss or HR or both. How can you use your new-found knowledge and skills to boost your personal effectiveness and performance in the job you're doing now and to prepare you for the next stage in your career?

Consider your future away from work, too. In all honesty, can your current employer help you meet your career aspirations? Your goals may have changed since you started the course; you may want to change career or go it alone, or start afresh with another company. If your employer sponsored you through your degree, did you commit to staying with the company for a given length of time after graduating?

Whatever you choose to do, stretch your new confidence and in-tellectual prowess. Work to achieve your potential, not to reduce it because your current role isn't right for you. That may mean cutting the strings with your current employer.

Questions to ask

- What do I want to happen next?
- Where do I see my career going in the next five years?
- How do I see myself doing this: with my current employer, with another employer or starting up alone?
- What do I need to do now to make this happen?
- How has my new degree status changed my CV and what I have to offer?

Re-write your CV for your next perfect role, or write a job de-scription for the role you really crave. What is missing from where you are now and where you want to be? Perhaps it's taking on a new project which will give you exposure to a particular experi-ence or new skill set. Ensure there are no other options open to you with your current company. Talk to your line-manager and HR department about the studies you've been doing and find out how the company can best use them. If you don't use them, you'll waste them.

'I want to work abroad!'

There's no doubt working abroad gives you tremendously different outlook to those who have not been so fortunate to experience such an opportunity. Recruitment companies who have an international reach often have advice on their sites about moving abroad. The website www.asia.hobsons.com has information on working in China, Taiwan, Thailand, Hong Kong, Singapore, Malaysia, Indonesia and Japan with market trends and industry summaries, and overall regional outlooks plus details of events in the area. Prospects (www.prospects.ac.uk) has numerous country profiles, incorporating details on the job market, international companies in the region you're reading about, language requirements, work experience, vacancy sources and visa and immigration information. Working abroad requires considerable research and preparation if you're to have the experience you want – they all vary greatly. See Further Reading at the end of this book for useful suggestions.

Questions to take into account

1   What do you want to get out of the experience?
2   Where do you want to work? Do you want to take the opportunity to learn a new language or improve existing language skills?
3   What do you want to do? Do you want to work for an employer in a job which will contribute to your career progression or simply go apple picking for six months?
4   How different do you want the culture of the country you're going to work in to be from your own?
5   How will your current qualifications be regarded in the country you plan to work in – will you need to get any additional 'top up' qualifications to meet their own regulations and criteria to work as a practising professional?
6   What visa requirements will there be? What happens about health insurance? What are the tax implications for you while working abroad and when you return home?
7   Can you do it under the auspices of your current or a future employer?
8   How long do you want to do it for?

Going it alone

Running your own business is about fulfilling your own dreams and not those of someone else. For many, working for someone else simply defeats the purpose of being alive. It's deadening to creativity, life, freedom, independence, fun, being able to work when you want at what you want. The amount of help for start-ups, certainly in the UK, is huge, from innovative centres where you can hire an office and share receptionist, secretarial and basic facilities at very inexpensive rates, to advice from business advisers, events and on-line sites designed to help you make all the right decisions.

Many graduates are entrepreneurs and choose to go the self-employment route. You can also set yourself up as a freelance, offering services and products by an hourly or daily rate, or buy a franchise in a region. You could work part-time to bring in the essential cash and then on your own business after those hours, but your attention and energies will be divided and it may be harder to focus.

You could consider buying a franchise, although if you are up to your eyes and ears in debt, this may be something for the future. The British Franchise Association (see Useful Addresses) is the only independent accreditation body for franchising in the UK. Franchises cover a wide range of areas from pet care to refill printer cartridges, accountancy and taxation services to training centres. There are also workshops and seminars to give you lots of advice and tips on choosing a franchise and running a successful business. Before you buy any franchise, check its financial status and insist on seeing the accounts from their head office.

Self-employment is not the rosy picture it often appears. Many small companies are being strangled by red tape and the compensation culture, and it can be a very lonely affair. Consider how you'll handle tasks such as planning your business' vision, writing a business plan, setting yourself financial targets, dealing with health and safety issues, accounting and financial responsibilities, taking on staff and keeping to the right side of the law, keeping the books and records, on-going business development, product and service development, dealing with the taxman, accountant and suppliers. It could be that your degree course has prepared you fantastically for this – all you need now is just the idea to set your business alight with activity!

Develop an idea, create a vision, do your homework and research the market thoroughly, and make your decision. Take advice:

networking clubs can help you talk to fellow entrepreneurs and help each other. There are programmes such as Flying Start to encourage graduate entrepreneurs (www.flyingstart-ncge.com) so investigate them fully.

Consider what you've learnt about businesses so far from your work experience and academic studies that might help you in your own business in areas such as business functions, customer care, marketing and selling, health and safety issues, branding, motivating people, record keeping and meeting deadlines. There are many courses and fairs for people who want to set up on their own, so look out for them in the local press and make the most of them and listen to the advice you're given.

Protecting your creativity

If you've come up with an idea you're really excited about, consider protecting it with copyrights, patents or trademarks. The Charter on Intellectual Property promoted a new user-friendly way of handing out intellectual property rights in 2005, written by an international group of artists, scientists, lawyers, politicians, academics and business experts. See Useful Addresses for further information on protecting your own ideas and designs by making full use of the support available to you.

To be ... a post-graduate or not?

If you need or want to take your knowledge and skill expertise to another level, you could enrol on a post-graduate course such as:

- Career entry related courses, for which you need no experience. For example, if you wanted to get into Leisure, Sport and Tourism, you could consider doing a post-graduate Recreational Management course, or if you wanted to teach, you could enrol on a one-year Postgraduate Certificate in Education (the PGCE).
- A course that will enhance your career progression, such as an MBA – usually for those who already have a couple of years' relevant work experience.
- Research-based studies, such as a PhD (Doctor of Philosophy) that take about three or four years full time to complete and

which can take you into the field of research, perhaps for a university, private organisation, institute or research project.
* A postgraduate degree which is taught, or which is taught and involves research. Business-related subjects include management, marketing, human resources, finance, banking, accounting and recreational management. In addition to a Business Studies degree, they will give you that extra specialist niche and qualification some employers may want. But then you may be better suited going on to work for a professional qualification. Weigh up your options and talk to professionals in the field before you decide what to do.

Some employers sponsor employees through degree and postgraduate courses and may even approach a university to create a bespoke course and qualification for their employees.

Equally, some people study a post-graduate degree for their own [career] development, perhaps part-time or online. People study post-graduate degrees for various reasons, to boost their career prospects or to simply increase their specialist knowledge and expertise in a particular area. Many students work for several years before taking a full-time post-graduate degree. By this time, they can envisage exactly how that study will fit into longer-term career plans, plus they've got experience to talk about when they finally come to getting that post-graduate job. Timing can be tricky, leave it too long and it may be too late to put impetus and fresh energy into your career.

Questions to ask before signing up for a post-graduate degree

1   How does this course take you closer to achieving your long-term career plans? Where does it fit within them?
2   Will a post-graduate degree substantially boost your chances of success? Will it really give you that edge over your competitors? What do employers think?
3   Are you contemplating post-graduate study simply to put off joining the working world for another year? (The longer you leave it, the harder it may be.)
4   What are the costs and what funding is available?
5   What have post-graduate students gone on to do after their studies? How do these paths relate to your aspirations?

6   What will it take to be a successful applicant and student?
7   What are your motivations for taking such a course? Entry into a new career, career progression.
8   What can you do to sell the benefits of a post-graduate degree to an employer? Many employers have enough problems understanding the benefits of an undergraduate degree, never mind the focus, rigour and academic discipline required to do a post-graduate one.

What evidence do you have that post-graduate study will enhance your employment prospects? Could networking and getting the right experience under your belt, perhaps by doing an internship, be as effective?

Reasons NOT to do a post-graduate degree

1   I couldn't think of anything else to do. (*A costly exercise in procrastination.*)
2   I'm so much in debt, a few more thousand won't make any difference. (*Yes, it will.*)
3   My professors thought it would be a good idea. (*Who's mind is it, anyway?*)
4   I like the town, and I wanted to stay on. (*So what's wrong with working there?*)
5   I enjoy student life, so thought I might as well stick with it. (*An expensive choice.*)

Further information on post-graduate studies

You'll find the official UK postgraduate database at www.prospects. ac.uk which lists the different courses available by subject, region and institution in the UK. You can apply online through Prospects, and even use some sections of the application for different courses which will save you time. In the UK, apply as soon as you can because the more popular courses fill up early – this means often October or November in the year before the course is due to start. The National Postgraduate Committee (www.npc.org.uk) represents the interests of post-graduate students in the UK.

If you live outside the UK, the British Council (www.britcoun. org) has offices throughout the world and can give you lots of information about studying and living in Britain. The National Academic

Recognition Information Centre (NARIC) (www.naric.org.uk) provides a service for international students who want information on the comparability between international and UK qualifications.

Short courses may be just the ticket

A short course may boost your employability and give you the skills you need to get that post you want. In the UK, you can find these at www.hotcourses.com; you could also visit your local college and private training companies to find out what they have to offer. A short course may also provide you with just the springboard you need to bounce into a new career. It should include a stint of work experience to give you confidence and practice, and the course tutors should also have strong contacts with employers in the sector, so they are worth exploring. When you have pinpointed what you want to do then, if you are lacking any particular skills, a short course could be just the ticket to close the gap between what you've got and what employers want. A career development loan (www.direct.gov.uk/cdl) may be last thing you feel like acquiring, it could provide you with the finance you need to fill that vocational skill gap and boost your employability.

Time out for golden sands, sea, sun ...

If you've been on the academic treadmill all your life without a break, you may feel like it's time for some time out, fun and rest. Increasing numbers of people all ages are taking time out and more (larger) employers are offering employees sabbaticals. They like seeing them return to the workplace refreshed, with a new confidence, fresh ideas, great soft skills and creativity. Gap programmes too are waking up to the fact that more of us want time out, and providing excellent opportunities for voluntary work and travel.

That said, you live your life once. The moment you stop experiencing such adventures as travel and facing challenges in life, you stop living and start existing. Some employers offer contracts to graduates allowing them to have a year out before starting work. You could go off travelling knowing you've got a job when you get back. In some areas where the market has taken a down-turn, and employers don't need a full complement of staff, this may be an unexpected offering.

If you plan to take some time out, you could look for a job before you go and try to negotiate a start date for when you return (assuming you will return); or you could travel and look for a job when you get back. This gives you more flexibility and possibly more stress as you wonder how on earth you're going to find a job and pay off your debts when you get home. One possibility is to consider overseas internships and training schemes. See Further Reading.

Unemployment ...

Not a very inspiring option, is it? So get busy.

Eight ways to pass the time while you're unemployed

1   Get relevant work experience, even if it's just for a week or a couple of days a week over a month or so.
2   Do voluntary work.
3   Learn new skills.
4   Travel.
5   Job hunt persistently and seriously.
6   Do something quite mad and quirky to make your CV stand out.
7   Study for a qualification which will give you on-the-job skills.
8   Get fit enough to run a marathon and then do it.

If your family are trying to help you but in the wrong way, be patient. They simply want to help and their intentions are good. Show them how they can help you by saying 'What would really help me is if you could...'. It could be that they could introduce you to someone whom you need to talk to about a career move into a specific industry.

Give your life a turbo-boost!

If you're currently sitting at home aimlessly with no defined plans or goals and no meaningful way to fill your day, it's time to change that. We all need to feel appreciated – it's a basic human need. If you're feeling that you've got lots to offer but no one cares, stop feeling sorry for yourself right now. It won't change anything. You need to change the way you're spending your day and how you're tackling your future.

Ten ways to climb out of where you are now and start walking purposefully to where you want to be are:

1   Find out exactly what careers help is available to you where you live now, whether you're still at university or not. Include universities and colleges in your area (whether or not you went to them), online services and private agencies. *Do it!*

2   Search out professional organisations which can help you build networks leading to introductions in the sectors you need; find out exactly what you will need to do to achieve that cherished professional status you want.

3   Talk to fellow graduates. What sort of business could some of you start up together based on your mutual interests and passions?

4   Build up a clear picture of the sector you wish to go into and be clear about how your skills, strengths and interests will contribute to it.

5   Talk to as many people as possible by going to where you know you'll find them outside the usual graduate arena, such as trade exhibitions and local networking events.

6   Brainstorm strategies you can use which will boost your chances of success, such as a willingness to move and live where the sector is strongest geographically. If you want to stay where you are, where the sector may be weak or even non-existent, you will need to be more flexible in terms of the sort of work you go for.

7   If you're still at university, explore the avenues for sponsorship with employers, even if it's just for your final year.

8   Find out what incentives there are to encourage graduates to work for small and medium-sized companies.

9   If you've been studying on top of working full time, talk to your employer about your future career aspirations (unless they are to leave the company) in light of your most recent studies. Don't wait for them to bring the subject up.

10   Set yourself daily targets and goals in every area of your life, not just your career. Life isn't just about work.

Summary action points

Move your thinking forward:

1   Which university or college runs the course in the subject I'm looking for?
2   What funding is available for me to set up my own business?
3   What initiatives are available that might be relevant to me and my career goals?
4   What do I need more of in my life? How can I get it?
5   What steps will I take next and how will they move me closer to my goals? What do I need to do to make them happen?

Chapter 4

Connecting with your network

The world's a network

Connecting to those in the know who can help you move closer to the things you want in life will enable you to enjoy a far richer life and career.

A strong, active network can open doors to decision makers and in turn enable you to reach out, help others and live a highly successful and fulfilling life. Whatever stage of life and career you are at, it will enhance your prospects of obtaining the openings and introductions you need. Highly successful people have a network of business associates, acquaintances colleagues and friends they can turn to for information, advice, introductions and help. You create your own luck and networks in life, however, and they are as active and useful as you make them. But remember that networking is also about helping those who *have* helped you, as well as those who *haven't*.

This chapter considers the *Who* question in a networking capacity.

- Who *can help me?*
- Who *can give me the support I need?*
- Which *websites will be most useful?*

Eight steps to good networking

1   An ability to chat and to be really interested in the other person; you need to be able to establish a rapport with strangers quickly.
2   Listening and questioning skills.
3   A get-up-and-go attitude – go out there and fight for your place in the world.

4   Follow through. Use the information you acquire, file it for future thought or action it or dump it, but *do* something with it.
5   Lateral thinking – does your contact know of anyone else you should talk to?
6   Respect! The person you're talking to has got to where they are by hard work. They believe in what they are doing and in what the job stands for. It may not turn out to be your niche or world, but respect them for what they love about theirs.
7   Being inquisitive and curious.
8   Accept feedback calmly.

You may not always like what you hear! Challenge the person giving feedback politely. *'This is a very tough industry and not many people make it to the starting blocks.'* Okay, so that may be the case, but clearly people *do* need to make it so you need to focus on that percentage – whatever it is – 5, 10, 20 per cent of applicants – and find out just what it is that brings them success. Focus on the people who've succeeded, not on generalisations that *'It's difficult, it's tough'*. It may well be but it's not impossible. Turn the negatives around to: *'It's difficult, but it's possible. It's tough but it's rewarding'*. Talk about the *'I can'* and *'I will'* rather than the *'I'll try'* or *'Maybe…'*. Ask people *'What is your perception of me?'* to get feedback on how you present yourself and how you come over. This will help give them something to remember you by. *'I met with a post-graduate who wants to work with small businesses. Sharp, good on strategy, really thinking things through. You should give them a call – might be able to help you…'*.

Understand what your career goals mean to you. What would the cost to you be if they didn't happen? Envisaging such an outcome can provide a terrific leverage to get you out of your comfort zone and make those phone calls and send the emails you need to make contacts. What are you prepared to do to in order to make sure it happens? Who are you prepared to talk to? How outlandish are you prepared to be in the way you tackle a situation? How far out of your comfort zone are you prepared to go to make it happen? Your passion for your career and what you want to achieve should inspire and excite you so much that you're prepared to do what it takes to sell yourself. Practise talking about your unique selling points (USPs) and what makes you different. True networking is only really effective when you push yourself out of the comfort zone and think out of the box.

A key benefit to your networking activities will be to create and build a strong support team around you. Each person on your team should bring you something different. There will be members of your support team you've known all your life, such as your family, family friends and your friends. Within that group, there will be one or two people whom you trust, perhaps just that little bit more than the rest. You know they will be open and honest with you and you also know you can handle any constructive criticism from them because it's fair and just. Then there are people who fill you with energy, a 'can do' approach, who could inspire you to great things. Perhaps these may include your peers at university; how often have you sat about and brainstormed an idea late into the night which is going to make you all lots of money and bring you fame? Keep in touch with those friends who enable you to unlock your potential and your creativity. There will also be the people you (secretly) admire and consider your success and role models. They may be a member of your family, perhaps your mother or father, or they could be a high profile leader in business, politics, the community, or someone with a 'go ahead' approach which fills you with energy and passion for your own beliefs and causes. Bring these people on board by studying their methods to achieve success. What did they sacrifice along the way to get to where they wanted to be? How did they focus? Why not contact them to ask them how they did it and what advice they have for you? Would they even act as a mentor to you? Finally, there are those who are not yet known to you – those people working in the sort of profession you want to be in, those who can advise you and help you along the way. It is here that the skill of networking truly comes into its own.

The benefits of networking

Networking is all about asking others to help you access information which will help you – or others – get to where you need to be. You can access information and decision makers. You can tap into those in the know who are most likely to know the answer you need – it's a bit like the 'phone a friend' lifeline on the UK television programme *Who Wants to be a Millionaire?* The contestants choose the friend who is mostly likely to know the answer to the question they are faced with, and it's the same here. You need to reach those beyond those you know and extend a line and call for information and help to those you *don't*.

This is the same in life. We all need the right people to call on in moments of crisis because we know they will give us the right support at that moment. We choose our friends because they have qualities we admire and enjoy. We elect to take some family members into our confidence as opposed to others because we know they have something slightly different to offer us, perhaps due to their life experience or their approach or attitude. As we go through life, we'll call on people at different times and there will be periods when we aren't in touch at all. Nonetheless, keep those fires of warmth and support burning because we know that when the time comes, we will need to know we can pick up the telephone and call them or drop them an email to ask for help, even if it's just a friendly ear. Just the same way, there are people who know they can call on us.

For the purpose of this chapter, let's consider how networking can help you in your career. If you brainstorm all the people you know, whom you've met or watched at presentations as they came into your university, you can probably draw up a long list of names (see Figure 4.1).

Fifteen ways networking can help you in your career

1   Acquiring relevant work experience, especially in highly competitive sectors where contacts are everything.
2   Getting help with your CV or application. What sort of CV do employers expect to see – fairly traditional layouts or something with a bit of creativity and flair?
3   Obtaining information about a career or organisation, or better still, an introduction to someone working in it who is working in the section or department you want to join.
4   Getting an idea of the skills, qualities and experience an employer wants and the personalities they recruit; would you be a good 'fit'?
5   Learning how a sector works, e.g. the culture, behaviour, dress, language and values.
6   Finding out the name of the best recruitment agency for you to talk to.
7   Getting advice on the best way 'in' to a sector or company.

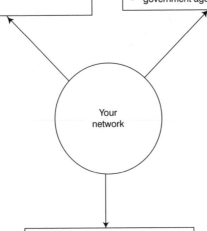

In the sector you want to work in:

- within a company
- across different companies in the sector
- universities to find out what's new and hot on the knowledge front
- university to university, if you're an academic
- professional bodies
- organisations devoted to the sector e.g. Arts Council
- cluster groups, on a national, regional and local basis
- graduate initiatives, e.g. Knowledge Transfer Partnership
- links between universities and employers

Networks dedicated to start-up businesses or helping graduates:

- the self-employed and small business networks such as the Federation of Small Businesses
- government bodies, e.g. BusinessLink
- cross-cultural networks and organisations
- organisations targeted at particular groups, e.g. Women In Rural Enterprises
- sector specific networks
- government agencies

Your network

Personal networks:

- leisure and hobby interests
- voluntary and public sectors
- community service organisations, e.g. Soroptimists (women) and Rotary International
- friends and family
- professionals, e.g. doctors, dentists
- product and service providers you use, e.g. banks, builders, garages, etc.
- school, college, university
- religious organisations
- fellow students – could you do something together?

Figure 4.1

8   Hearing of projects an employer needs doing but does not have the resource internally to undertake which you could then volunteer for.

9   Getting tip offs when a job comes up – many companies advertise their vacancies to staff first on their notice boards or company intranet.

10   Acquiring the opportunity to shadow someone by going in for a couple of days to find out what life is really like in a company or performing a role.

11   Finding out what roles are available for new graduates.

12   Finding out where is the best place to look for vacancies.

13   Discussing the industry overall, its strengths, weaknesses, opportunities and threats; the pros and cons of working in it and how it is structured.

14   Hearing about what opportunities there are for someone who is qualified; what will life be like then? What doors will professional qualifications open for you?

15   Hearing about how they manage full-time work and study for professional qualifications and have fun and live life at the same time.

Many people don't push their network into unknown areas so never truly reap the benefits networking can bring.

The danger of networking with fellow graduates is that if you're both in the same boat, you may simply spend time and energy bemoaning the current state you're in, which won't change anything. So if you're talking to a fellow graduate, have a good moan for five minutes and then spend 15 minutes brainstorming in which you can both change the situation you're in for the better and bounce ideas and contacts off each other. One of those ideas could be the breakthrough you've been looking for.

Get pushy and ask for help – most people will be delighted to help you

---

Five steps to pro-active networking

1   Identify what you need to know or what sort of people you want to meet and why they are important to you.

2   Identify the people you *do know* and imagine on paper what their network would be like.

3   Make contact and ask for advice and help. If someone has referred you to a contact, mention their name.

4   Approach people you don't know but can find more easily through relevant professional organisations and trade associations.

5   Think big and laterally and you could connect to thousands of people worldwide at a stroke. The key is to secure introductions to the people in the right place.

Along the way, if you meet someone you get on with particularly well, why not ask them to act as a mentor to you?

Mentors have been there, done it and got the t-shirt. They can be an invaluable source of help, advice and contacts and many mentors get a great deal from the process themselves. A mentor is likely to sit down with you and talk about your goals, aspirations and how you can get there. He or she should be experienced people in the field and sector. They will help you to stay on track and keep focused on your goals, so you are likely to achieve them more quickly. They will probably be flattered you asked. You can have a mentor in any area of life, from exercise and fitness to finance.

Professional organisations

Professional bodies exist partly to help promote the public's confidence in the professions they represent. As such, membership of a professional body may be essential to practice. They also help members and new entrants into the field to have satisfying and fulfilling careers, access to the right training and networks, and meet the challenges and opportunities that come their way. Many such organisations in business and finance related industries are listed under Useful Addresses at the end of this book. They will have advice for you, the new entrant, the career changer, the mature student and the young professional. They can point you towards areas of their website which may be particularly relevant to you. Their sites may cover such topics as demonstrated in Table 4.1.

Discussion forums are very useful to see what the hot topics are so that you can prepare for them prior to job interviews. Many use the forums to seek careers advice from their peers. A lot of

Table 4.1

• A register of practitioners and their areas of expertise and specialism, often with their contact details	• Career case studies
	• Learning and education
	• Useful links
	• Information about the profession as a whole
• Events taking place at which members, associates and affiliates may gather	• Library services
	• Annual conferences in the UK and abroad
• Jobs search	• Salary calculator
• Online forum groups	• Services available to the public
• Latest industry news	• Vacancy listings
• Latest publications relevant to the industry	• Advice line on pricing issues
	• Setting up on your own
• Research	
• Information for the public on the body, its standards, ethics and training	

organisations are allied to international groups, which could expand your network at a stroke in the EU or further afield. Most have local networks, with regular meetings, events, training programmes and newsletters, visits to businesses and social gatherings. Many meetings are held with a meal – breakfast, lunch or dinner or simple drinks – to give members the opportunity to talk to each other and catch up, meet new people and exchange ideas, information and advice.

Go on – attend a meeting in your area

It is in the organisation's interests to show you goodwill and interest and yours to represent yourself in a professional manner. Dress in business attire – suit and tie – and practice good social skills – a warm, firm handshake, a smile and lots of eye contact. Ask questions – what people do, who do they work for, what sort of clients do they have? If they give you their business card, follow it up with an email saying something like, 'It was nice to meet you – would it possible for us to meet up? – I'd love to talk you further about ...' Be ready to talk positively about your course, the projects you did and your career plans. Mention articles you've seen in the press or online which show you're up-to-date and show enthusiasm and interest. Find out before you go about any initiatives in your area which are running to strengthen the relationship between graduates and small employers – it could just help swing the mind of a small employer to give a graduate like you a chance, if only he or she had some guidance on how to make the most of you.

If the thought of attending such a meeting fills you with horror…

Why not contact the person in charge of your local group to explain that you're coming along for the first time and to ask for someone to look out for when you arrive to introduce yourself to? There should be someone there whose role it is to welcome new members and make them feel at home. Look out for them when you arrive, ask them to introduce you to someone who is fairly new to these professional gatherings, too, or someone who is working in a specific area that you'd like to get involved with. Find out in advance who will be there so that you know who to look out for and prepare some questions in advance. Visit their website to find out more about them. Be interested and you'll soon forget your own nerves. Remember that you're with a group of like-minded people who may well remember what it's like to start out. They're on your side.

Ask for an information meeting

Professional organisations can be a great way to find the right lead and name in a company you want to work for – and to learn of companies you never knew existed. They can provide you with the opportunity to get an information meeting, by which you simply meet someone working in the industry to get their advice. Mention how you came by their name. That can give you a lot of credibility because personal referrals can go a long way. Identify specific questions to ask before you go so that it is clear you have given the meeting some thought and prepared well for it.

Join your alumni

Do it now, before you move on and the years slip by. You'll find details on your university's website. Try tracking down past alumni who are working in sectors you want to join to ask them what would you would be expected to do on the job, in your first year, and how might your career progress after that? What advice would they have for you? Can they suggest anyone for you to talk to? What do they like and dislike about what they're doing, and what they see the challenges are from the point of view of their career and life. What appealed to them about the organisation they joined and how has the partnership fared so far? Where do they see it going in the future?

Academic groups

Academics network across the world as much as professionals in the business field. They attend conferences, listen to papers, give presentations, undertake joint research projects, compare notes, research, debate, argue, discuss, discover and invent. They talk on the phone, they email and they have their own networks across their universities, research institutes and other relevant organisations. They live and breathe their subjects, and they're encouraged to work with business, whether they like it or not, and to create a far more entrepreneurial spirit in their departments and students. Don't forget them in your search for the right career and position.

You may well decide that academic life is for you. Visit websites such as www.jobs.ac.uk for information on jobs in the higher education sector and check the institutions' own websites for vacancies. As well as academic posts, universities also need staff in areas such as finance, marketing, public relations, administration, student support, human resources and facilities and building management.

Networking outside your sector

If you're running a small business or freelance service, you need to decide how to promote your services. In this instance, you could consider attending local events put on to help business people network and exchange business cards so that they can pick up on each other's services and how they may help businesses. The government networks with responsibility for helping entrepreneurs should have networking events in your area, often specialist in nature, enabling you to meet with like-minded people. You need to explore what networks are available in your area and on the Internet and assess which ones will be most appropriate for you.

Why not meet a local small business person who has a fairly high profile in the community and call them to see if you can meet them or pick their brains about which networking groups they've found to be the most effective and helpful? They should be flattered that you approached them.

Go out there and immerse yourself in the fabric and make-up of those working in the sector you want to get into

Aim to build up a very strong understanding of the world you want to work in and seek to identify who really knows the local scene and has an influence in it. They are the people you want to meet to see if they can help you along the way. There may be cluster umbrella groups who are dedicated to the sector you wish to join in your region. A number of bodies work with small businesses, such as the Federation of Small Businesses, the Small Business Service, Start-Ups, BusinessLink, Growing Businesses and Chambers of Commerce and the Forum of Private Employers. They can all signpost you in the right direction. These will enable you to make friends and potential clients, customers or employers over the Internet. Examples are Everywoman.co.uk and ecademy.com.

Do it successfully

Open-mindedness and generosity is crucial, but be discerning too. Listen to what people have to say, and then assess the information and feedback you're getting against what's important to *you* and your criteria.

Ten more steps to successful networking

1   Don't assume the information you're getting is current. Don't assume those you're talking to are up-to-date. Go that extra mile by checking with the professional bodies and trade associations.

2   Guard your safety. If you're meeting someone, do so in a public place or in their office premises. Visit the company on the web to make sure their address is valid. Don't give too many personal details out over the Internet or telephone.

3   Present yourself to the highest standard you can using business behaviour and language, not text speak. Examine your image and wardrobe from head to toe in front of a long mirror at home in your interview suit. If you need to, ask your bank to extend your overdraft to buy a decent outfit. Remember that every time you open your mouth, you're selling yourself.

4   Use networking to take on strategies and solutions which will put you ahead of the rest, whether you're looking for a new job or starting and developing your own business.

5   Networking is a two-way process. When people help you, see if there is anything you can do to help them. Look to build on the relationships you develop. Treat others as you would like to be treated yourself.

6   If you are at a networking event, spend about five minutes or so talking to the person you're with and then move on. You are all there to meet as many people as you can, so don't feel guilty about closing the conversation. *'It's been nice to meet you. Shall we exchange cards and move on?'*

7   Think about the impression you want to portray. What perception do you want the people you meet to have of you? Do you want to come over as someone who takes their career and chosen field seriously and passionately, or as someone who's out to have a good time? Are you portraying yourself to be someone who can be trusted and thinks before they act or speak and someone who will be loyal to their current employer, who won't talk down past employers?

8   Don't give the impression you're a job hopper and just keen to move from one role to another. It costs employers money to recruit staff and they won't be too impressed if you stay with them for a year and then you're out and about networking for a new opportunity. Word may get back to your current employer, especially if you live in a small community. Be discreet if you're already working and looking elsewhere for opportunities.

9   Set yourself goals for each networking opportunity. Divide your networks in groups and give each group a goal for the week or month, e.g. *Attend professional networking meeting on Tuesday 23rd. Aim to meet Tony Johnson from AC Accountants and Bill Turner again to discuss possible options.* Measure your success. Is there anything you're doing which is working really well for you and, if so, how can you build on it?

10   Keep in touch with people in your network. Email them from time to time to ask how they are and how things are going. Tell them how their advice and information has helped you and offer to help them in return. A network is only as active and alive as you make it.

What about websites?

You can access careers advice and information online and in person. Wherever you are, visit or contact your local university's careers service and find out what help is available to you as a new graduate. Be specific about the help you need. Know the questions you want answers to. Go into careers interviews knowing what you want to cover. Be honest with yourself and others – this is not a test. If you're from the European Economic Area (EEA), you can get free personalised advice services if you've graduated from university in the last five years and you're seeking advice on work and study in the UK through the Prospects website. You can email a careers consultant and have your CV checked.

Prospects

This is a truly amazing site (www.prospects.ac.uk), with lots of information on subjects from work experience and internships to CV writing. Prospects offer a free personalised advice service to all graduates and students – you can talk to graduates online, and there are regional services in the UK and Ireland.

Hobsons

Hobsons is a huge careers resource. You can benefit from their global approach, with information on job hunting, job applications, interviews, assessment tests and even study-to-work information. You'll find industry profiles, regional outlooks, details on international opportunities and an A–Z of employers. Visit www.hobsons. com for more information.

Sector specific

Websites in themselves can be invaluable, particularly if you use them to signpost you in the direction of other sites. The Links sections are often overlooked but make good use of them. Many are quite specific about working in an industry, such as www.efinancialcareers. com with 'Day in the Life' of sections and 'Sectors explained'. Also, check out www.insidecareers.co.uk/, which covers accounting, engineering, banking, actuaries, IT, logistics, management consultancy, patent attorneys, purchasing and tax. If you register, you get access to graduate vacancies, company profiles, expert careers advice, plus information on application deadlines, careers events, and university visits. Finally, most professional bodies have websites and they are listed at the back of this book.

Business coaches

Career and business coaches help you identify what is important to you, what you want to achieve and what you need to do to make that happen. They also help you address any barriers or obstacles ahead. Career coaches usually coach people by telephone, although a business coach may want to come and coach you at your place of work. Check that your coach is qualified and trained and find out what experience he or she has before parting with any money. If you're not sure about where you're headed, a career coach can be very helpful in helping you work out your future direction while ensuring that the things you hold dear in life – such as work–life balance and time for the family – are held true.

Networking is for life!

Networking can be very helpful in all sorts of ways such as:

1   finding specialist expert health advice;
2   locating the estate agent who will really get your house sold fast and is always the first to hear of houses coming onto the market;
3   getting your children into the right school;
4   looking after ageing relatives and making the system work to your advantage;
5   volunteering to give something back;
6   asking about hotels for that special holiday next year;
7   meeting new people at the pub, in the gym and through your interests;
8   learning something new and keeping your life fresh and active;
9   having fun and giving something back at the same time;
10   making life easier.

Summary action points

The way you network at every level can affect the flavour and fabric in your life so make it a priority.

1   What network groups are there in your area with which you can make contact and get involved? List them and make that first contact.

2   Find out if they have mentors to help people like yourself who want to get into the sector. If they do, ask if you can be allocated one.

3   Contact five people in your network. Ask if they know of anyone who could help you. Arrange to meet for a coffee to catch up with them or organise an information meeting.

Chapter 5

Hunting out the right opportunity

So far, you've ascertained what you want to do – now you need to work out how and where you want to do it.

How important is the 'where?' to you?

What factors are driving your decision in terms of where you live? Many UK graduates are moving abroad in search of high quality lifestyles and career opportunities: Spain, the USA, Canada, Australia ... well, why not? What have you got to lose? The following can all impact on your career and lifestyle, but which option in each line is important to you? Table 5.1 gives you an idea of choices to consider.

Other factors which will impact on your lifestyle are your access to cultural activities, sports and leisure interests, the make up of local people and quality of life in the area. You are unlikely to find somewhere which meets all of these criteria so some degree of compromise will be required. If your career matters to you above all else, you'll move to where the sector is strong and growing fast as opposed to where it is non-existent. For example, the financial services industry is strong in London, Frankfurt, Paris, Milan and Zurich but also smaller cities such as Lugano and Edinburgh. In Asia, Singapore and Hong Kong play key roles, while in the USA, New York, Chicago and Boston are important financial centres. If you have dependants, moving away may be more difficult, so talk to them about the options. They may secretly be ready for a move, too.

Every sector will have its hot spots and weak spots within a given area. Each region has its growing industries and those in decline. Find out where your sector's hot spots are by looking at the government's sites relating to trade and industry, the economy and sites

Table 5.1

Near friends	Same town as friends	Ready to make new friends and keep in touch with old ones
Close to family	Living with parents	Irrelevant – we email and text and they can visit
Cost of living low	Cost of living irrelevant – salary will match	Need to keep this in mind – must find out what living costs are
Opportunity to live cheaply to pay back loans	Have bills, but then doesn't everyone?	Not as important as the job itself
Sector I want to go into is strong in the region with lots of employers	I'll take my chances – I want to stay in the city I did my degree in. I'll take what I find	I'm ready to go to the other side of the world to get the job I want
Staying in home country	Want to go abroad	If the job takes me abroad, so be it
City	Town	Countryside/rural
Irrelevant – the job comes first	Have a strong preference for where I live	Am absolutely living in this city regardless of opportunities
Short commute to work	Commute is irrelevant – it's the job and employer which matters	Willing to commute within reason

such as the UK Trade and Investment at www.invest.uktradeinvest. gov.uk/. It has both sector and regional information. In areas of traditional and declining industries, redundant skills and depleting resources, Regional Development Agencies (RDAs) are responding by leading and creating initiatives in such areas by regenerating them, boosting learning opportunities and facilitating skill acquisition and start-ups. Government bodies such as the RDAs will tell you which sectors are expected to enjoy strong growth or experience a shrinkage – labour market intelligence can be very helpful. Cluster groups and localised graduate websites (see Further Reading at the end of this book) may direct you to useful local networks.

Analyse the sector and size of company in it

Does the sector consist mostly of small and medium-sized business-es? If so, you may be best networking to meet them or sending in a carefully thought through and well-presented letter of application and your CV to the boss. Spell out what your qualifications mean – smaller employers are less likely to be up-to-date with changes in education. Make life easy for them. Larger companies will probably put you through deadlines, application forms, personality tests, telephone interviews, assessment centres, person-to-person interviews and more. A Graduate Recruitment department will probably handle everything. Understand how companies recruit – it will save you time.

The size of the niche area or sector will make a difference as to how competitive it is to get into. There may be 30,000 PR companies in the UK, for example, but 300,000 banks. Clearly it will be easier to get into a bank than a PR company.

Discover and explore the SME market

The small, medium and micro-business sector takes longer to research but they have a lot to offer. AGCAS (www.agcas.org.uk) has a DVD *Big Opportunities in Small Businesses – Graduates in SMEs* exploring how graduates and employers can work together.

Seven reasons to work for a small company

1   You'll probably enjoy more responsibility across a broader range of areas; it's easier to take advantage of any new roles which arise.
2   You may have faster career progression.
3   You'll have a finger on the pulse and know what's happening.
4   You'll learn more and probably apply a range of the knowledge you learnt at university, as opposed to focusing on one area.
5   You can become resilient in developing your career – there won't be any HR or personnel section to help you do this. If you work for a small company, you will need to be pro-active in seeking out the training you need.
6   You can put your entrepreneurial skills to use without taking risks yourself.
7   There's a less structured and hierarchical work environment, faster decision-making processes.

In the UK, most companies – 99 per cent plus – are small and micro-businesses. Put yourself in their shoes as *business* people. They've probably put a huge amount of time and money into it yet they still go through peaks and troughs of work. One week, they will be pushing their backs to the wall at three in the morning every night, while the next they will be gloomily staring at the phone or email systems, wondering where the next piece of business will come from. They need more staff for peak busy periods, and very few in others and that need can change from one hour to the next. Bosses in small companies probably spend too much time and energy and focus on the 'doing', rather than delegating to give themselves time to focus instead on strategic planning and business development. They are being strangled by legislation such as health and safety and employment laws. Every time he or she takes on a new employee, there are also new worries, such as will this member of staff head out on maternity or paternity leave shortly after arriving? Will they fit in with the rest of the team? Will there be sufficient work long term to justify another member of staff? Visit any small business networking sites you can find in your home country to get a feel for the issues concerning them. Could the freelance be about to enjoy a boom in business? Could you (and your peers) market some of the skills you have on a freelance basis, such as doing research and analysing facts and figures, or market research designing questionnaires? Is there a particular aspect of your university life and experience to date which you can package and sell? Could you set up a service with a fellow graduate?

What initiatives are available to encourage employers to take on graduates?

In the UK, RDAs are encouraging universities and businesses alike to retain skilled talent in their area and working to raise small companies' awareness of how graduates can benefit them. There is a strong connection between the skill levels in an area and the quality of working opportunities and lifestyle on offer which is why huge efforts are being made to regenerate those areas which are lagging behind. These bodies are also trying to encourage inward investment which should create more employment opportunities. You should consider initiatives such as the Knowledge Transfer Partnerships (www.ktponline.org.uk) which enable graduates to undertake a project within a company while acquiring management training at the same time, and don't forget internships and work experience programmes (see www.work-experience.com). Many regional graduate careers service providers (see Useful Addresses) offer work placement programmes and schemes designed to boost your employability.

Institutions, too, are responding to graduates wishing to stay in the region after completing their degree. As mentioned in Chapter 1, there are regional graduate careers services (online) in the UK and these are listed under Useful Addresses at the end of this book. They show what help is available to you, advertise vacancies, organise events and have work placements plus lots more.

Look for signs in the national and local press. What is happening around you which could impact on recruitment?

If a company wins a big contract, how are they going to source it? Could you offer to work on a temporary basis or freelance, if you've got the skills they need? Why not send your CV in on spec to the person who is mentioned in the press. Focus heavily on what you can do and make it as work-related as possible and give them a clear picture of what you can do for them.

Do you want to work to improve society or the world?

There are many choices open to you, depending on where and how you want to make an impact and a contribution. The Charity sector is booming. Modern charities need professionals – lawyers, accountants, HR managers, press officers, researchers, IT staff, overseas managers, chief executives – so even if you join the private sector straight after graduating, you can work for a charity later. In fact, this is often your best route in: to get your professional qualifications and some experience behind you and then go off and change the world. In the UK, certainly, there has been an improvement in the working conditions experienced by those working for charities and the pay gap between them and other sectors is closing. Many charities are relocating from the more expensive parts of the UK (London and the South East) to other areas.

The larger players offer structured graduate recruitment schemes, but most smaller charities do not. If you want to work for a specific charity, show willing and do voluntary work, preferably for the charity you want to work for, to prove your worth and your commitment. Find out who the decision makers are so that you can network with the right people. The sector is for you if job satisfaction and contribution are more important than money.

Many graduates are working in the fair trade revolution, or setting up social enterprises to boost causes they feel strongly about. The latter are not-for-profit organisations, but they really can make a difference. You could also contribute to another country's development, working with the people who live there. Examples of work volunteers may include teaching, care and community, medicine, business, journalism, law and sport. See Useful Addresses at the end of this book to tap into these.

Working for the community

From housing associations to local government, there are opportunities with graduate training schemes, management training schemes and other ways 'in' without the graduate tag. The UK government has increased the number of jobs in the sector by nearly 600,000 since coming to power in 1997, most significantly in those areas where it has a strong foothold in power. Opportunities range from working in the police force, health service, education, management, trade and enterprise. In addition, there are bodies such as NATO, the UN, the EU and international aid agencies.

Finding suitable employment opportunities

Employers use a range of methods to recruit employees and you should use a range of methods in your job hunting. Consider how employers recruit. They could enlist freelances or temps to save them taking on staff long term. But they also have a range of other options available to them, including working with links with schools, colleges and universities through careers fairs and presentations, their own websites or those of agencies, advertisements in the local press, looking at on-spec applications, finding students through work experience, internships and secondments. They could spread the net wider, hooking potential recruits in through agencies, the national press and specialist trade journals; some are even using radio and television adverts.

Seven steps to hunting out opportunities

1   Identify where you want to work.
2   Run a search for all the relevant employers using all the means at your disposal, including Kompass, Dun and Bradstreet, yell. com, local Google and specialist agencies.
3   Use your local library which should have sector reports, books and information about the local area, trade and national magazines, phone and trade directories.
4   Register for any email alerts with online agencies to pick up new jobs which come in that might interest you.
5   Careers offices may also produce vacancy bulletins. In the UK, these include: *Prospects Today* and *Graduate Employment and Training (GET)*. Once again, these are UK related and will be targeted by many graduates or undergraduates, so don't rely on them as your only source of hunting.
6   Look to your university for help. The department you studied with at your university may be working in partnership with an employer you particularly want to 'get in with'. Employers may approach your old department directly to recruit students.
7   Use your network. When a vacancy becomes available, most employers look at their existing staff to see if anyone could do the role. If not, they will ask their staff if they know of anyone who could do it.

Going through recruitment companies

Recruitment agencies are selected by employers to find recruits for them. Many employers have long-standing relationships with agencies, so agency consultants build up an extensive knowledge of what the employer is like to work for and what sort of career path candidates can expect upon successful application and starting.

Agencies offer various services to their candidates, including help with CVs (although some agencies have their own particular CV format to send to clients), and profiling so that you can work out what sort of work would suit you best. Your consultant should have a clear idea of trends in the sector, and how your career will fit into it, and he or she should have strong links with the industry. Many offer training and some run networking evenings. It's essential to remember that your consultant is human too, so treat him or her as you would like to be treated.

Online recruitment has become big business. Many online agencies and professional bodies offer the facility of receiving email alerts, enabling you to receive notice that new (relevant) vacancies are available. Newspapers and trade magazines also have online vacancy boards and often send newsletters. You may also be able to post your CV on some sites for potential employers to view.

Go places where you know you'll find employers

For example, you know professionals will be present at professional body meetings and careers fairs. Careers fairs and exhibitions may be specialist or generic in nature and not necessarily organised by university careers services but by local services. Some fairs may be specific to starting up your own business and include a plethora of organisations who can help you. At any careers event you may expect to find some or all of the following.

- Employers, private and public, the Armed Forces and charities.
- Training providers.
- Time out opportunities such as working holidays abroad, gap experiences. These are usually there to promote the options they have as Time Outs, but there's nothing to stop you finding out what's the best way 'in' if you want to work for them.
- Recruitment agencies, usually out to recruit potential consultants at graduate fairs rather than signing up people on their books for a job search.
- Providers of (student) services such as travel and insurance.
- Key graduate careers services such as Prospects and Hobsons.
- Government agencies such as the Job Centre Plus.
- Any initiatives which are taking place with a graduate focus such as Knowledge Transfer Partnerships.

Fairs enable you to compare what each stand-holder has to offer. Whether you are attending a trade show or careers exhibition, they will be more fruitful and productive if you plan for them in advance and identify what you want to get out of them before you go. You can acquire a full list of Graduate Fairs in the UK on the Prospects website at www.prospects.ac.uk. Some employers run initial interviews there and then and decide whether to put you forward for the next stage. Don't forget sector specific events, trade shows and exhibitions. Take a generic CV with you for consideration which is not targeted to any one employer but may be slanted to appeal to a specific sector. Find out if there are workshops running alongside the event which may be useful.

Plan for a successful event

When you approach stand-holders, an introductory chat about their company and what it's developing and working on can quickly lead to a sentence or two about yourself and your career goals. Regardless of whether you're going to a trade show or careers event, tips for a successful show include:

- Pre-register online to avoid lengthy queues.
- Identify the people you want to meet. Visit their websites before you go. Visit their stands *first* while you're fresh and full of energy.
- Create a business card for yourself to hand out. Put your contact details (email and mobile number) and *Willing to re-locate* on it if you are. Also, your last educational qualification on one side with niche areas; and the sort of company you're looking to work for for plus skills you have to contribute on the other.
- Prepare questions to ask in advance, so that you don't stumble over awkward introductory waffle, but sound clear, confident and interested. *'What advice do you have for someone in my position?'* and *'What job hunting strategies can you suggest I use?'* can be two helpful questions to get insider information and give you other routes to follow.
- Ask open questions. *'Do you recruit graduates of any discipline?'* is a closed question requiring a simple yes or no answer; you won't learn much. *'What degrees do you particularly look to recruit?'* is an open question and hard to answer with a yes or no. Open questions give you more information and enable you to engage the person you're talking to in further conversation.
- Don't start off by asking *'What can your company do for me?'* or *'What can your company offer me?'* Promote yourself as someone who has a lot to contribute to the right employer.

- If someone looks busy, wait until they are quieter later. You may spot them having a quiet coffee in the café areas and you could approach them then, ensuring first of all that it's okay to interrupt their solitude! They may be more thankful to sit down than anything else. Be aware that others really will want to get away from it all.

- Talk to people in the café areas. Get chatting. Make some small talk about the fair – *'What a great opportunity to meet people!' 'What a great venue!' 'Isn't it good to sit down?' 'Are you here as an exhibitor'? 'What does your company do?' 'I'll stop by and see you at your stand!' 'Could I contact you next week and ask for some of your time?'* Smaller companies may not have a stand, but you might bump into a representative from one if you start talking to people in the café areas.

- Many fairs have separate areas for exhibitors to feed and water themselves, but you may also meet some people who can point you in the right direction. *'You really should talk to …'*

- If you get stuck talking to people who are being negative about your general situation, *'There are too many of us graduating!'* politely say goodbye and wish them luck and walk away. Focus on what you *do* want and ways to increase your chances of succeeding in getting it. Sitting and moping isn't one of them and it will certainly get you down.

- When the event is over, walk away and reflect over what you've learnt about the opportunities available and yourself. Bring together action points and carry them through. Business cards create dust if unused; you want them to create results.

- Write and thank the people you met at the show by email or letter. If you have a web CV, you can attach the address under your contact details at the bottom.

Heading to other shores – working abroad

Ten questions to ask include:

1 What is the local job market like?
2 How do employers recruit staff there and what is involved in the recruitment process?
3 How should I write a CV for that country and what should I include?

4   What organisations and websites can I turn to for advice and information, such as Prospects and Hobsons?

5   Does my professional body or trade organisation have any relevant links in the country I wish to work in and what support can it give me?

6   How will my current qualifications transfer and will they be accepted? Many professional bodies are working with other countries across borders to ensure the smooth transfer and recognition of qualifications from one nation to another.

7   How does the working environment differ and what is acceptable behaviour and what is not?

8   What level of job would I have with the competences I have got?

9   Will I need to take additional tests to prove my competence in my new country before I can start work?

10 Where in the world will my knowledge and skills be needed in the future?

Put *Willing to Re-Locate* on your CV or business card but be prepared to actually do it. If you're focusing on one country and you satisfy visa requirements, say so on your CV or covering letter (see www.workpermit.com). Look out for events and newspaper supplements promoting life or companies abroad. Use your network to help you get work overseas. Read journals and newspapers. Make use of embassies and State employment services such as http://europa.eu.int/eures. The European Job Mobility Portal is one of the places where European candidates can see an employer's vacancy and employers can multi-search for CVs which may meet their needs. It links the public employment services in Europe and helps people take up work in other member states of the European Economic Area (EEA). It has lots of information on jobs, learning, labour markets, health and registering for work when you arrive, and working conditions.

You could also sign up with a recruitment agency that has international offices or connections, or go through an organisation offering placements abroad, such as GAP, or simply do it yourself. Don't forget to tap into any twinning arrangements and Chamber of Commerce organisations (www.chamberonline.co.uk/). These have links to trade organisations and research they've undertaken into markets abroad. Their site has details of all the UK Chambers, overseas Chambers in the UK, British Chambers of Commerce overseas and

Council of British Chambers of Commerce in Continental Europe. It also has an excellent export zone and business services on offer.

Returning home later on

The various locations you choose to work need to be kept in mind when you're considering where to settle later in life. Sooner or later, you may want to come home. Watch for any trends or new laws or regulations there which may impede on your ability to return when the time comes. Consider the financial implications for your future. How will working abroad affect any pension due to you later in life, for example, be it state or private? Read *Working Abroad, The Complete Guide to Overseas Employment* by Jonathan Reuvid (see Further Reading).

Your next steps

1   List employers in the sector you wish to work in to research in the country you want to work in.
2   Develop a short list by researching them. Continue your research through the web, careers fairs, finding out about their products and services, your network, news items.
3   Who do you know, or which sector networks could you tap into, to acquire an introduction to these companies? At this point, your networking efforts will really pay off.

Why not go to places where graduates *don't* normally look for work to stand out from the crowd? While all your peers are heading for the same avenues, do what they wouldn't think of doing. While they are all gunning for the big corporates, what could you do to steer your own course that nobody else would think of doing? When you come across a company which really excites you, consider the organisation which lies behind it. Someone must be making everything happen. Why shouldn't you be a part of it?

Moving things forward ... do you, don't you?

Find out more about the organisation and its career opportunities, but don't confine your research to the company's website. Search further and wider for any mention of it in the local, national or international media. Most employers try to provide as much information as they can about their organisation to job hunters so that the latter can ensure they are applying to the right sort of company for them. Why not see if you can get in touch with someone appropriate at the company to see if you can visit and look around, and talk about the opportunities available?

Questions to ask of a potential employer

1   What is its mission and what does it want to do and achieve? Does it excite you?

2   What messages does it give you about its values and what it deems to be important? What values does the organisation or company portray in its advertising, literature, image and brand? Look for evidence that it upholds these values. Do they excite you?

3   What is the size of the organisation and how will that impact on the way people work and the opportunities within it? What does it say about how to apply for work?

4   Where is it located? Is it spread over a number of sites?

5   What is the structure and hierarchy; is there just the one company or are there a number of subsidiary companies within one group?

6   How is it organised? A small company may have one person looking after IT, marketing, sales, web design and HR which would put a generalist business degree to excellent use; a large one will have a department of people for each of these elements enabling you to focus on one area.

7   What is the company's financial position? If it is not healthy, your career there may be short. What are its strengths, weaknesses, opportunities and threats?

8   What sort of people work for it? Look at employee profiles. What do they get involved with outside of work? How do they describe themselves, the company and their roles?

Find out what the company is doing to be innovative and competitive. Where does it see itself going and what is its place in the market? If there is no evidence of such activities, ask yourself whether the company will exist in five years' time? Or can you contribute to the company's overall business development and expansion? Careful research into its finances and diplomatic questioning at interview time can help you assess such a state.

Nine key questions to ask yourself

1 What could you contribute to this organisation in terms of skills and qualities?
2 Is this the sort of place you'd look forward to walking into every Monday morning?
3 Could you see yourself working for them in five years' time?
4 Can they offer you the future you're looking for?
5 What would you need to do to make the career progress you want to enjoy and what support would you get from the company?
6 What is the organisation's view on work–life balance and what specific examples are there to support their view?
7 How could you secure a foot in the door?
8 Is there a vacancy right now you could apply for or will you need to make contact on spec?
9 What actions are you going to take next and when?

You could multiply the opportunities before you if you consider working for an organisation short term, perhaps on a contract basis – plenty of professionals do – to get experience and get your foot in the door. Part-time work will leave you free to job hunt for the role you really want, or to develop your own business while bringing some money in. A small company may not have enough work to warrant taking someone on full time but it may offer you part-time work. Think laterally and creatively when you're job hunting.

Starting your own business

There is more help around than ever before for those with an entrepreneurial spirit but still too many start-ups fail for lack of sufficient advice and research. The BusinessLink network in England helps small businesses and start-ups. Visit www.businesslink.gov.uk to find your local link. There's information on setting up a business, writing a business plan, accessing funding, growing your business and even selling it on. There are also links to the sister organisations in Scotland, Wales and Northern Ireland.

Consider initiatives

Aside from Flying Start (see page 42), other national examples of organisations helping people to set up on their own include Shell LiveWIRE, the Prince's Trust, Start-ups and the Prime Initiative for the over 50s (see Useful Addresses at the end of this book).

Ten questions to consider

1 What's your vision and what do you want to achieve with this business?
2 What are your products and services?
3 Who will your ideal client be?
4 What do you need to get up and running, e.g.:
   * somewhere to work from;
   * equipment needed to set up (you may have a lot of this already);
   * computer/lap top/ipod;
   * communications – Internet, phone, fax;
   * marketing and publicity materials – possibly a website, business cards, brochures, membership of professional and business networks;
   * insurance, professional indemnity and public liability;
   * life and critical illness cover (discuss with a financial adviser), health insurance;
   * training;
   * a salary/wage?
5 Where will you get funding from?
6 Who can support you?
7 What new skills and knowledge will you need?
8 Who are your competitors?
9 What will your niche and unique selling point be?
10 What research do you need to do?

Be alert to opportunity

Watch the world carefully and keep up-to-date with events and trends. Are there any booming economies which would benefit from your skills and talents? Events which can be disastrous for some people provide huge opportunities for others. For example, a company makes 500 people redundant. That's unfortunate for the 500, but a great business opportunity for careers coaches and redundancy advisers. Similarly, the Olympics in Beijing in 2008, London in 2012 will offer great opportunities for people with the right skills.

Summary action points

Move your thinking further forward:

1   What are agencies in the region doing to encourage businesses to take on graduates, particularly those in my sector?
2   How much do I know about the work I want to do and how to get 'in' to it?
3   What initiatives are available to those who want to set up their own business?
4   Where are most of the employers located in this sector?
5   Which other areas are showing a rapid growth?
6   What would the sector look like if I were to draw a mind-map of it?
7   What am I doing to enjoy life and have time out while I'm working towards my goals?

Chapter 6

Proving yourself

From scholar to worker

One minute you're a student and the next you're not. You may choose to have some time out or get going on your career straight away, but whichever path you take, there's a big difference between the two.

Making the psychological switch

There is quite a switch from being a student to becoming an employee or self-employed, because the impact of your work and how well you do it affects other people, as shown in Table 6.1.

The 'learning to do' referred to above relates to those things you cannot be taught until you start work, such as product knowledge specific to the organisation you join. But, at the very least, employers want to know that you know how to behave at work and that you understand what work is like.

The more you understand what it's like to be at work, the easier the transition from scholar to worker will be.

At work, you'll still get the person who does it all at the last minute, those who are indecisive, bullies, patronising or negative. You'll have to manage people who spout 'We've always done it like this', and see no reason to change. And there are those who are moody, sulky and lazy. You'll also have your power-crazy people who are highly competitive, the workaholics who have no life outside the office and you'll need to deal with them all. Your skills and talents in motivating and managing people will be well tested as you move up the career ladder, and you will need to be a manager, mentor and coach to bring out the best in others. You'll need to use your influencing and persuading skills to encourage those around you to

Table 6.1

As a student		As an employee
Studying	*and*	Working
Being a student	*and*	an employee/employer
Learning	*and*	Doing or learning to do ...
Student responsibilities	*and*	Responsibilities at work to-wards: team; clients, customers; company/employer; your own colleagues, peers
The hours you choose to work	*and*	The hours you're expected to work
Holidays	*and*	Average 4 weeks holiday – in the US, probably 1 or 2 weeks in the first few years
The way you dress and behave	*and*	The image and behaviour that's right and appropriate for work
Long-term personal goals	*and*	Vision, mission, targets need the goodwill and motivation of every-one on board
Rules and regulations in your university	*and*	Employment laws, health and safety, professional regulations
Meeting deadlines – it's just you that suffers	*and*	Meeting deadlines – other people are depending on you
The pace of life – you can dictate it	*and*	The pace of work is dictated by the industry and demands of cli-ents and customers. Your day can change dramatically on receipt of a phone call. People expect fast responses. Are you adaptable and flexible?
Your performance – it affects just you	*and*	Your performance can affect that of your team and the company – it can clinch a deal, save the company money
You can control pretty much most things in your life	*and*	There are many things you can control but equally there are many you cannot

see the benefits of what you want to do. Your experiences at university will have given you a good start in speaking up for yourself and getting along with a huge variety of people from all different backgrounds and with their own aspirations.

Support it with work experience, and you can put the above skills into place and make the psychological switch. To make that more effective, you need to live, breathe and perform in a real live work situation.

The extra-curricular approach

While you were or are at university, you may have indulged in extra-curricular activities, such as socialising, drinking and quite a few other things best left off a CV. Equally, you'll have activities which demonstrate your initiative, motivation and drive through activities you *can* put on a CV.

Go volunteer!

The simple act of volunteering itself gives you invaluable opportunities to put your soft skills to the test and prove their effectiveness. You can put your foot in the door and get noticed. You'll feel appreciated, needed and fulfilled and you'll have fun volunteering with like-minded people. It's also a great way to expand your network. Many universities and employers recognise the value of voluntary work as a way with which to develop skills and capabilities. Why not find out if a local charity has a project it needs doing but doesn't have the resources to do, or come up with an idea for a voluntary organisation which would make a difference to them and then implement it? It could be a great way to show employers what you can do from start to finish *and* practice working with a client. If you're setting up your own business, you could do your first assignment for a charity either for free or a heavily discounted rate in return for a testimonial to put on your marketing literature or website.

Analyse all those extra activities

List everything you'd done during your university days and you'd be astonished at what you've achieved. Do it now, including the formal and informal. For example, you could have spent a lot of time helping newcomers settle in during the first few weeks of term, but not in any official capacity. This would have helped you develop your people skills, listening, questioning, probably boosting morale, sign posting people in the right direction, communicating, etc.

Rank the transferable skills below in order of your strength, 5 being the strongest (see Figure 6.1).

Now find evidence for each one looking through your list of extra-curricular activities, voluntary efforts, work experience, academic work. Pick out the examples which would be most relevant to the role you want. Which are your strengths? If you were asked about your weaknesses, how would you respond? What strategies could you say you were taking to tackle these weaknesses?

Have you made the most of university life?

University days offer the chance to create something – anything you like – out of the process. It's effectively time to live the life you want, the way you want. Yes, you've got studying, part-time

	5	4	3	2	1
Organising/planning					
Communicating, orally					
Communicating, written					
Learning					
Creativity					
Decision making					
Self-motivation					
Strategic planning					
Handling change					
Problem solving					
Team working					
Leadership					
Adaptability, flexibility					
Self-awareness					
Commercial awareness					

Figure 6.1

work, and all the pressures of being a student, but you've also got an opportunity to really go mad and do something different, if you want to. Employers will be looking to see how you occupied your time during those years and how you benefited from them. How have you developed? And what skills have you acquired during your studies?

Once again, delve into your university years.

- Identify all the subjects you covered. Can you find consistency among them? Do they build a story and theme throughout your university days?
- How did you study those subjects? What were the modes of learning and what have you learnt from them as a result? Seminars, tutorials, lectures, presentations, visits, projects, essays, debates, assignments are all relevant to the workplace.
- What do you know about? Organisations, business, accountancy – whatever you studied, you have the theory. How many examples can you show of times when you've applied that theory in practice?
- What systems are you competent in, e.g. use of email, research on Internet, creating a database, packages which are relevant to the career you want? List them so that employers recognise what you can do. Give live examples of the times when you have used them, with deadlines, timescales, what you were looking to achieve.
- Describe how you work through each of your transferable skills. For example, when given a task to do, how do you complete it from start to finish? Do you follow the same process each time?
- Will any parts of your course count towards accreditation for professional qualifications?
- What gaps are there which you should fill?
- How can you demonstrate your enthusiasm and motivation?

Once again, skills you learn in academic life transfer over to your working life (see Figure 6.2).

Effectiveness and high performance at work is built on the right attitude, a professional competence and approach, product and sector knowledge, a *drive* to make things happen and soft skills. At university, you develop academic and soft skills through various academic and extra-curricular activities. To progress your career,

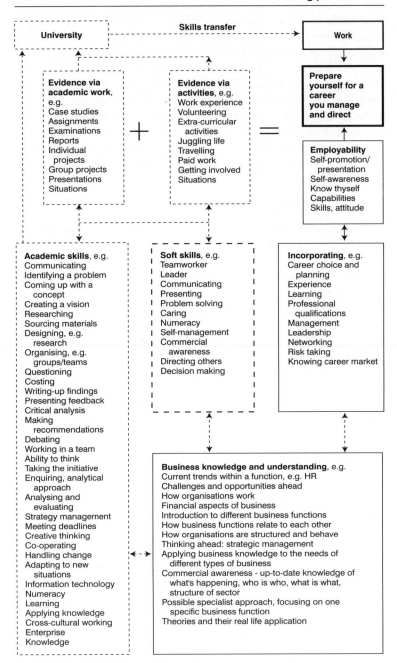

Figure 6.2

you need continued exposure to different experiences, professional qualifications and management roles which continue to expand your capabilities and push back your comfort zones and you also need to build on your soft or transferable skills. (A financial adviser, for example, must be able to explain the different financial options open to clients who know nothing about finance in language they understand.) Self-awareness, self-promotion and self-presentation is also important, along with keeping abreast of career developments and news in your field. Figure 6.2 shows how university and work link together incorporating all these elements.

This extends beyond work!

Throughout your life, both in and out of work, you'll need to manage a number of ingredients, as shown in Table 6.2.

The ability to manage yourself and others impacts on your ability to be personally effective in work and life. For example, if you have children, you'll need to motivate them and get the family working as a team on projects to create a cohesive family unit. There will be times when you need to manage your own temper, when they do something which drives you to distraction for the hundredth time. Similarly, you will need to manage your client relationships at the office. If someone asks you for a piece of work which you know you cannot do within the timescale they give you, you will need to manage that and talk to them about it. You've learnt to manage people, situations and life at university and in your past life experience.

Who are you?

This is not just about your qualifications and experience to date. They certainly contribute and play a part, but this is more about how you arrived at the whole-rounded individual you are now. It's not

Table 6.2

Yourself	Information technology
People	Resources
Teams	Materials
Time	Projects
Money	Deadlines
Your energy	Research
The client's expectations	The facilities around you
Your future	Your suppliers

about 'Well, I completed my UCAS form and made my six choices, and then sat and prayed that I'd get in to my first choice!'. It's about, how did you come to apply at all? What and who moulded your decisions and what did you need *within yourself* to get to where you are today? What resources did you pull out of your body, heart, mind and soul to make your degree happen and how can you build on them and use them to maximum effect throughout your life? Who did you work alongside as you strove to achieve your mutual goals? (*That's teamwork!*)

It's also about your values, and what matters to you. After all, you must have chosen the path you took for a reason. So what lies behind and within you, what makes you tick, what drives, inspires and motivates you. What challenges and dramas have you faced? How have you tackled them? (*That's problem solving.*) If you wrote your life story, what particular achievements would you want your readers to know about? What journeys would you want to tell them about? How can you show them that you've turned your plans into action? Have you done a stint of travelling or juggled study and work at the same time? (*Shows adaptability and flexibility, planning and organisation.*) When have you really had to knuckle down and make things happen? Were there times when you kept going when everything else seems to be going against you? How many times have you failed at something – anything – and you've tried and tried again until success came your way? (*Persistence, motivation, drive, resilience.*) What changes have you dealt with in your life; if you've driven them yourself how have you tapped into your drive and energy and passion to make them happen? If they happened outside your control, how did you handle them? (*Resilience, ability to ride through change.*) What negative experiences have you been through that you've learnt from? How could you show a stranger the person you truly are, as opposed to a bunch of qualifications listed neatly on a page? (*That's written communication, persuading, influencing, expressing.*) What sort of person would they see? It's these qualities that you need to bring out in your CV or interviews when applying for jobs or courses. (*That's self-promotion.*)

It's also about those things which prompted you to make the choices you have in work, play and leisure, in your friends you hang around with. (*That shows what motivates you.*) What circumstances have you grown up in which have influenced you, your actions, your choices and the messages you've taken on board about yourself, life, the opportunities ahead? (*Decision making and action planning skills here.)* What have you done to challenge them? *(You don't settle for just anything and the status quo!)* What have you done to help yourself? These sorts of things have all contributed to make up the person you are by influencing and moulding you over the years. It will also show you that being successful – however you define success – takes tremendous hard graft, self-discipline and continual, sustained effort. Without ingredients such as these, success all too often feels hollow, empty and unsatisfying. Look at all the times you've been proactive and what the results were. Look at the opportunities you created for yourself by getting off your back-side and making something happen. *(Taking the initiative.)* If you want to be successful in the way you envisage success, you need to do that again and again.

However you've studied towards your degree, be it full time, part time or by distance learning, take time to congratulate yourself. Sure, go out with a group of friends and sink a few drinks. But take time to quietly, independently and proudly assess what you've achieved and, crucially, the characteristics in your personality, the motivators and drivers which empowered you to success, such as persistence, determination and curiosity. You've had the endurance to get through a degree, however long it took. You developed the ability to network, form working relationships fast, to take responsibility for your own career development and learning and to be resourceful. You've tacked obstacles which were in your path and overcome them.

Acknowledge your strengths and resources in writing

Writing down your strengths and resources will give you lift, especially if you're feeling low. Whatever stage of life you're at, you'll need to draw on all your resources to create the future you want. Get ready to dig deep and raise your energy levels, standards, focus, persistence and drive to a higher level to propel yourself into making it happen. Finally, you'll be able to tell employers more succinctly what lies behind the person you are – and the person you want to be, thereby selling yourself more effectively. Self-presentation and promotion is an important skill at work today.

The power of work experience

Work experience strengthens your hand in the employment market, particularly if it is targeted towards the career you intend to follow and structured in such a way that you can learn and put the theory you have learnt on your degree course into practice. Employers can see you in action for themselves: the way you walk and talk, think and act, behave and motivate, initiate and inspire, work and apply your new found knowledge. They want to see how effective you are and how you achieve results. In fact, employers rate work experience and internships as a highly effective way to find graduate recruits. There is a plethora of such schemes on offer throughout the year which run at Easter, Christmas, in the summer or for a full 12 months. Entry is often highly competitive, requiring the same professional approach and strategy to achieve success as job hunting. The small and medium enterprise (SME) market in its own right can give you the chance to get your foot in the door. There may be a scheme running in your area to help companies and graduates benefit each other. The National Council for Work Experience has a lot more information on its website (www.work-experience.org). Also look for opportunities to gain experience through professional bodies and trade association websites.

Work experience should play a central role in your sales strategy when you start job hunting. It shows that you know what you're letting yourself in for. You can talk about your experiences and achievements at interview and demonstrate both the job-specific and transferable skills you've used. You can prove how you can be relied on to get results, to make things happen and to achieve. You can prove your passion for and belief in what you're doing, that you've got your hands dirty; talk the lingo, understand the frustrations, challenges, issues, opportunities and threats.

If you've found a work experience opportunity on your own, turn it into a constructive learning time. Identify what you want out of it and what you have to offer before you approach an employer. Find out if there is a project you can do to practise specific skills and put your course theory into practice. Observe closely and ask the right questions, and you'll acquire an insight into how the different parts of the organisation pull together as everyone works to fulfil the mission or vision set out in its profile.

You can pick up the language relevant to the sector and the organisation or company itself. Listening skills are important if you're to pick up the language and way of working specific to the business. Each one has its own terminology relating to its systems, protocol, meetings, hierarchy, and many have their own intranet. Dress down Friday may mean jeans and trainers in one company; in another, it may not exist. Work experience gives you insight into how companies function and helps you make those all-important contacts. *'I've got a friend who works in PR. Shall I mention you to her? She could give you a call for a chat.'*

What behaviours and practices do you need to elicit to make your 'it' happen?

- ◆ Be very determined. Push for your corner, but remain polite.
- ◆ Get focused.
- ◆ Be prepared to sacrifice something else in your life so that you can give what you really want the hours it deserves. True friends will understand if you can only meet them once a fortnight or once a week.

Start behaving and immersing yourself in the field you want to be in

If you're job hunting, devote as many concentrated hours a week to the task as you would as if you were working. Thus, if you're planning to work full time, spend 35–40 hours job hunting. Keep your ambitions and goals at the forefront of your mind, or they will lose their prominence as the years go by and seemingly it will take more effort to make them happen. This is particularly important if you consider yourself to be presently in a 'lower level' role. Position yourself to get out of it, either by moving or staying put or one of two things can happen (see Figure 6.3).

Join relevant professional organisations and network groups. Talk to people about what you want to do. Go places you are likely to find potential employers. Give out your business card as you go. If you are sold on a particular career and you're just looking for the right opportunity, why not enrol for your professional qualifications if you can and start studying for them?

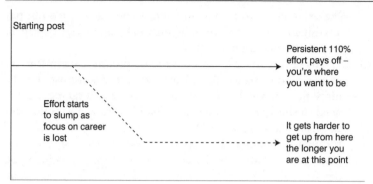

Figure 6.3

Temping your way to a career

Like work experience, temping gives you the opportunity to show what you can do. But can you take the initiative and turn what could be a dull temping job into a really constructive learning opportunity and experience?

Seven steps to getting 'in' to a company through temping

1   Specialist agencies tend to focus on a specific sector such as media, PR, education, office management, accountancy, finance, nursing, law, engineering, construction or management. If, however, you simply want to get more experience of the workplace while you make your mind up about what you want to do, high street agencies cover many sectors. Some have specialist divisions working in graduate recruitment; a visit to the company's website will help you assess its strengths and focus.

2   When you sign up with an agency, behave and dress as if you're going for an interview. The agency needs to know they can send you out to represent them. Your consultant should spend time with you assessing your skills, competencies and interests. If they don't, ask yourself how well they know the employers they're sending your CV to! Towards the end of your initial meeting, ask how and when you should keep in touch with your consultant. Recruitment can move quickly, so

she or he needs to be able to contact you quickly. Do not pay anything to an agency to find you work; employers pay agencies for finding them recruits.

3   Try to get two-week, three-week or month assignments together in one sector to enhance your CV's consistency. Be more flexible when it comes to the first few assignments; you need to show you can be trusted first before you get choosey.

4   Look for ways to put the knowledge and skills you've acquired through your university experience into practice in the company you're with. Ask the company for projects to help you demonstrate the skills you have to offer, even if you do them voluntarily. Include them on your CV.

5   Reflect weekly on the new skills and knowledge you're acquiring in terms of your competence at work and yourself. What assignments have you enjoyed best so far and why? Which environments have you thrived most in? What have you achieved in each assignment? Get feedback on your performance from your agency and the employers you've worked for. What perception are people getting of you?

6   Update your CV regularly and send it to agencies you've signed up with so that they are sending out your most recent one. Give timescales, budgets, deadlines, anything which shows the circumstances in which your achievements were arrived at. How have your efforts made a difference?

7   Consider what do you need to start doing to make the overall experience more effective and to take you closer to achieving your goals. What strategies can you employ to make these happen?

Many people temping will not bother with the above strategies. Work is exhausting enough without thinking about careers every minute of the day. But this is where that 100 per cent commitment and effort pay off. Yes, you're there to do a job – but you can turn that to your advantage too. And remember, working at the bottom of the organisation is a way great to learn how the various parts work.

How do you take time out to go for interviews?

Companies are paying for you to be there and do the job they need you to do, not to keep disappearing for interviews with other companies who may be their competitors. If you keep calling in sick, this makes you look unreliable in the eyes of the agency *and* employer. So what's the answer? Many employers are prepared to interview people first thing in the morning or late afternoon. If you need to arrive late or take off early, try to ensure that you work extra hours the day before or after at your temporary assignment. Give your temporary employer as much notice as possible. Give 100 per cent and your temporary employer won't want to lose you. If the agency you're temping with is also working to find you that right permanent post, talk to them about your dilemma. How do they suggest you handle the situation?

Don't wait for doors to open for you. Get out there and start knocking on doors to connect to the opportunities you want.

If you want to set up a business while working, do it while others sleep

Consider the number of wannabe writers who rise at 4.30 a.m. to write in the hope they can pack in the day job once they hook a deal with a publisher or get that e-book up on the web. If something is important enough to you, you'll *make* time for it, schedule it in and, inevitably, sacrifice something along the way to achieve your goals and ambitions. Keep the dream alive and work to turn it into reality. Nobody said it was easy.

Learn from others you deem to be successful. How do they do it?

You can learn a lot from those who are where you want to be. A motivating and inspiring read is Sarah Brown's book, *Moving On Up*, with advice and stories from all leaders in various sectors on how they got to the top and what it takes. Seek out those who are where you wish to be. Use your network to enlist get-ahead strategies. Talk to insiders. They've done it. They're working in the sector you aspire to join. Learn from their advice and let them know how you're getting on. Would they act as your mentor? People love to talk about themselves and many will see it as a compliment if you ask their advice.

Talk to other graduates who are now on the career ladder that you want to climb onto. How did they do it? What can you learn from that approach? What would they do if they were you? Who would they suggest you talk to, approach, contact, network with, send your CV to? Who's business or department is expanding, growing or taking-over? Can you mention this graduate's name? What skills and qualities do they think employers are looking for in their recruits? What will make you stand out and give you that special 'wow' factor? And before you leap in to write out an application and CV, or complete a form online, ask yourself the *Who am I?* question to ensure that this employer is what you want; and then you can decide how to mirror these factors in your application.

You can learn both from graduates you come across accidentally, throughout the recruitment process at assessment centres, open events and so on, but also on websites such as the excellent www.doctorjob.com, which has a great resource in comments made by graduates on a whole range of subjects including assessment centres (often company specific), interviews, work experience placements and so on. These comments make inspiring and comforting reading as you learn that you're not the only one who may have become frustrated, irritated and despairing.

Summary action points

Turn your experience from an academic one into a work-related one which means something to employers and gets you in the right mind-set.

1   Look to see how you can start living the working day so far as possible.
2   Identify steps you can take which will bring you closer to the role you want.
3   Review your progress to date in areas such as: your own self-awareness and how far that has come; your picture of your career and life in the next three to five years; how your network has changed; and how far you've researched potential employers (or courses) to apply to.

Chapter 7

Applying some self-promotion

The next stage, as you prepare to sell yourself, is to consider questions such as:

* What can you do to boost your chances of success?
* What can you control? What is outside your control? (For example, you can control the time you spend job hunting and where you choose to job hunt.)
* How can you use your application to demonstrate the skills you have?
* What if you like where you are now and want to stay?

If you respond to an advert in a newspaper, you can control the quality of your application, but you cannot control the numbers of applicants applying for the same post. You can choose to demonstrate your ability to communicate clearly and present your case well by submitting a well thought out, easily read and well expressed application. Equally, you may just complete the questions and press the 'send' button without any further ado.

This chapter will look at selling yourself, once you've identified a small number of employers you wish to work for. If you can be flexible in terms of how you work that organisation, such flexibility will give you the chance to put your foot in the door and prove yourself.

Do you want to stay where you are?

It may be that you are already working for that employer and want to stay. Talk to the company, and most specifically to those who make the decisions. Be ready to outline your contribution so far and your unique selling points. Record and mention your achievements. In short, prepare as if you were going for an interview.

Remember, enlist several ways of job hunting – don't put all your eggs into one basket. Aim to do something with each method at least once a week.

Once you've identified an opportunity or course you would like to take or an employer you would like to work for:

1   Determine what you need to do next, be it applying for a job online via a questionnaire or application form, or in writing, and whether a CV is required; or whether you should make an unsolicited application.

2   Identify any deadlines so that you can work out what to do when, giving yourself time to review your application and have it checked before submitting it.

3   Pinpoint the skills, knowledge, acumen and attitude your potential employer needs by researching their organisation carefully and analysing their values and vision, goals and targets; the language they use in their literature and on their website; check those you must have in order to be considered for the role.

4   Note the questions you need to answer and find the evidence you need to paint the picture of your capabilities and aspirations from your research, life resources, characteristics to date, work experience, voluntary work, travel, leisure, team efforts and projects.

5   If you need to include a CV with your application, write it out until you are comfortable with it; produce a one page letter of application and anything else required. In your one page letter, highlight the skills and experience you have which are relevant to the role you are applying for, and explain why the company you are writing to appeals to you.

6   Before you submit your application, have it checked by someone else and copy it, so that you can refer to it before interview.

If you have to complete an application form, and (decide to) send a CV with it, it is tempting to put 'see my CV' on many of the answers. Many companies scan applications and such an answer will result in your CV heading to the bin. Application forms give recruiters an opportunity to compare applicants, so apply the 110 per cent effort rule as opposed to 80 per cent This rule also needs to be applied persistently and with rigour throughout the job hunting process.

Submit an outstanding application, not just an excellent one

In the recruitment process, there is one winner, i.e. the person who is selected, who will stand out over the other applicants. The person who is selected will have probably given an outstanding performance from start to finish; the others may all be excellent, but in a competitive world, there is only one winner. So if you're going to put yourself a cut above all the other applicants, you need to make yourself stand out as an outstanding candidate.

Get physical

Finally, it's a competitive world out there, so prepare yourself to fight for your part in it. Exercise daily to sharpen your mind and body – the results will be apparent from your added energy and increased focus. Minimise the rubbish you eat and drink, including alcohol. Mental agility exercises will help you improve your ability to think on your feet.

Put yourself in the recruiter's shoes

Think about what you know about the company and the sector, and the role they are recruiting for. What are they looking for? What do they want? One retail recruiter offering retail management training programmes wants: 'Customer service – it's vital for us. They need to be able to relate to the general public and to the staff who they'll be responsible for. We need to see that in a CV'.

Do your homework on the application process

There are plenty of specialist books on the market regarding CVs, application forms, applying online, assessment centres and the interview process and these are all listed under Further Reading. Raise your standard over all the other candidates: invest a few good hours in reading and learning from books such as Martin John Yate's great classic, *Great Answers to Tough Interview Questions*. At the same time, read books on recruiting which have been designed for large and small employers to find out where they are coming from. Then find the middle ground. (See Further Reading at the end of this book.)

Get practice in tests

If you know that tests will form part of a company's assessment of you, ask your careers service for a practice run, or find practise tests online. Have a go beforehand. Know what you are letting yourself in for and get practised in handling questions, managing your time, focusing on a task for a short period of time. It's that 110 per cent effort again, as opposed to the 80–90 per cent one. The website www.prospects.ac.uk enables you to get your CV checked, talk to graduate employers and practice online personality and aptitude tests. Do it! What do you have to lose? Remember, ask yourself why the employer is including this test and what they are looking for.

Five golden rules to kick off

1   Use a professional email address. Always put your contact details at the bottom and use an appropriate header in the subject box, such as Graduate Opportunities, and address it to the right person. You can find that out on the company's website or by calling the switchboard.

2   Check your mobile and email regularly for messages. Recruitment can move quickly.

3   Your application could be read in as little as 20–30 seconds by many recruiters, especially the larger ones. Make it easy for them read; use bullet points, not prose. Explain your educational qualifications – spell out subjects you covered and the skills you've acquired.

4   On your CV, use a short opening statement of 30–40 words to describe your career aspirations, relating them to the role you're applying for or the company you'd like to work for. Throughout your CV use adjectives to give the recruiter a flavour of your personality. Describe honestly hobbies and interests and any achievements you may have. Paint a picture of the

person who lies behind the CV or application form. 'I want to see some creativity and individuality come through', says one recruiter.

5 Give the reader an idea of the scale of the projects or achievements you've worked on to paint a picture of what you've done, using numbers, targets, deadlines, results, feedback and percentages. These all contribute to a mound of evidence showing how personally effective you are, and they show that you can get results. Your degree may already have given you exemptions to certain professional qualifications, so if that is the case, say so. In addition, be specific about your use of communication and information technology, such as spreadsheets, word processing, online databases, email and Internet research. You can take your evidence from life activities from Table 7.1 below.

Consider the skills and qualities an employer wants. For example, have you:

* Worked with a team to a tight deadline?
  The client wants this presentation tomorrow morning at 8 over breakfast.
* Solved a problem (on your own and with a team)?
  Here's the problem, and the solution
* Managed projects, events or people?
  Such as you'll do when they recruit you.
* Handled studying, working and fun?
  You are human, after all. They don't want to take on a robot.
* Initiated projects or activities?
  'Let's start a careers forum online about this.'
* Delegated a task?
  (This doesn't mean asking your mum to do your laundry.)
* Motivated other people?
  (This doesn't mean asking your mum to do your laundry.)

Table 7.1

Study	Extra-curricular activities
Work experience	Volunteering
Voluntary work	Travelling
Paid work	Projects
Leadership roles	Business activities at university/
Membership of societies	college

+ Taken responsibility?
  I'll find a way to do this.
+ Showed resourcefulness?
  How did you fund your trip around the world?
+ Showed flexibility?
  Tell us about a time when you had to change your plans at the last minute to fit in with a situation.
+ Led others?
  'We can do this ... so who's going to do what?'
+ Debated a point with someone and influenced them?
  (Not on the merits of going down the Union for a pint.)
+ Analysed information and developed a strategy from it?
  Well, here are the figures and it looks like there are more graduates on the job market this year which means that ...
+ Taken responsibility for your own learning and career development?
  I know where I'm going. I learn best by watching others and then having a go myself.
+ Been driven to achieve results?
  I sold 750 tickets over the weekend in the Union for our concert – my efforts really were effective.

Make CVs personal and relevant to the company you're writing to

A CV should include headings for areas such as:

+ Contact details (at the very top, easily spotted);
+ Academic history (most recent first), pinpointing the most relevant aspects of your course to the employer and mentioning any exemptions from professional qualifications the course has given you, if relevant;
+ Work experience; aim to build a picture of the experience you have acquired and your achievements;
+ Overall achievements;
+ Any positions of responsibility;
+ Interests and leisure – keep it brief and honest;
+ Personal details – for example, 'Willing to re-locate' if you are; a clean driving licence; marital status and age (use date of birth as opposed to age in years).

Limit your CV to two sides or less. Send it by email or by post on paper (good quality white A4 with no gimmicks, designs, wrinkles or coffee stains). Don't put 'Curriculum Vitae' at the top – employers know what it is. Consider the sector you want to work in. Some – such as the professions – accountancy, banking, law, etc. – expect conventional CVs. Others such as the media expect candidates to be more creative. Ask people in your network what is expected of applicants and whether they can give you any examples.

Many applications go straight into the delete folder or waste bin, since they are riddled with spelling errors, hard to read and poorly researched. Others get a glance and perhaps go into a 'think about while reading the rest' pile. Some are easy to read and relevant, and then one or two will make the employer think 'There's that one line which makes me sit up and think, wow – I've just got to meet this person'.

What happens after submitting your application?

For larger firms, kick-off may involve sending in your CV or completing an online or paper application form, or perhaps doing an online psychometric test or personality questionnaire. Some personality questionnaires enable employers to develop a target profile for which an applicant's characteristics can be measured online, such as find and fix faults and numerical-reasoning skills. Many employers then run initial screening by way of short telephone interviews with candidates, asking a standard set of questions before deciding who to put forward. This stage may be dealt with by an agency for of the company. The person calling you may try to pick holes in your statements and push you into a corner – a great chance for you to show off your debating skills.

As said before, for the small or medium-sized employer, you will probably need to send a CV and accompanying letter of application and then attend for an interview.

Tell your housemates that you're job hunting; ask them to answer the phone with greater courtesy than usual. Keep your details, a pen and paper by the phone so that you can immediately recall your application, what you can offer the company, and handle the call appropriately. Put your unique selling points and a few main details at the top so that they stand out. Include a generic CV with your life history on it so you can quickly refer to grades you've obtained, if asked, or find information required.

I don't just give 100 per cent. I give 110 per cent

Can you show evidence that you go the extra mile? In these days where every added value makes a difference – as you'll discover with your own clients if you run your own business – the right attitude and approach count. They make a difference. Can you think of examples to show that you went the extra mile, took on extra responsibility and volunteered to help someone, showed a desire for excellence and pride in your achievements?

Look at your potential: where do you want to be?

Where do you see yourself in five years' time? Who do you want to become? Increasingly, job prospects relate to the person you are and want to become (your potential), hence the heavy emphasis on psychological tests, assessment centres and even handwriting analysis in the recruitment process. It is not a good idea to say 'I'd like to be running my own company' or 'I'll be travelling on a year off' or 'I'd like to be in your job'. Show ambition, but not at the expense of the interviewer, unless you're applying to a large company where there are clear ladders of progression. An employer will also want to know that you're a stayer. The recruitment process is a long and costly one, so they won't want to take on somebody who intends to leave within a year plus of joining, unless you move up their ranks.

This is a question that employers like to ask when recruiting and many job hunters think, 'Wow. I don't even know where I want to be next week! Why are these guys so hooked on this question?' The thing to remember is that recruiting and training staff cost money and time. Employers need to know where your level of ambitions and drive are taking you, what your values and aspirations are and where you see yourself going. They need to look at the staff they are recruiting, to assess the spread of talents and skills they need and how you might fit and contribute to fulfilling their long-term vision, now and in the future. If you're looking at a large global organisation, for example, they may have had to forecast their recruitment needs over a year ago. But they may also equally recruit on an ad hoc basis, as the need arises, particularly if they are a smaller company. 'What could this person do for us starting from Monday?' is the likely question a small company will ask but they too will be looking for people who can grow with and contribute to the organisation.

The fact that you have a degree shows your commitment to learning and developing yourself and realising your potential. An employer can see that by evidence of your conscious decision to go to university and get a degree when you were free to do anything you wanted to. What's more, they know you have the ability to learn and juggle life, study and work. So your degree shows an employer that you can progress. They can build on your strengths, weaknesses, skills, creativity, leadership abilities and management material. They can train you, probably promote you, give you a team of people to manage and expect results from you. They may provide financial and timely support for you to study towards professional examinations but they need to know that you can and will stand the pace of working relatively long hours during the weekday and studying at night. They'll look for the evidence in your application from start to finish.

More importantly, you and any potential employer need to know that you're right for each other. This is very much a two-way process. If you are not right for each other, it's far better to acknowledge it immediately. The way the organisation is structured may not enable you to meet your aspirations. Learn from the experience and move on. The same applies if you're considering going on to further study. You need to make sure the thing you are applying for, be it a course or role, is right for you and your long-term plans.

Prepare to show your commercial awareness

Continue to research:

- The sector you want to work in: industry news, who are the movers and shakers, who's who, which companies exist in it?
- The make-up of that sector and how the organisation you want to work in fits within it;
- How the organisation stands out from its competitors. What makes it different? Be able to talk about their products and services, their culture and ethos. What are their unique selling

points and how do those compare to the organisation you're applying to?

* The appeal of the company you applied to. Why did you pick them over all their competitors?
* The qualifications involved (assuming you intend to study for them). Does your degree exempt you from any part of the qualification? If so, mention it.

Throughout your application, look to demonstrate your commercial awareness by having a keen business insight into the companies you are researching to apply to, keeping up-to-date with the opportunities and threats and trends in the sector, understanding where the organisation fits into the sector and how it is performing. Check share prices on the day you go for any interviews and read its last few annual reports to see how far it is to reaching its goals or vision. Pick up on the bigger picture by researching it throughout the Internet, talking to people who may know about it. Find out who its competitors are and what their strengths are against its own. Demonstrate you understand how organisations are organised and function, and that office politics enters into life at work – wheeling and dealing to get the best for your department and subsequently your career.

Show how you can benefit the company

Demonstrate that you have researched these points:

* What is the company's mission and vision?
* How does it expect to achieve that?
* What will it need to achieve it?
* What sort of drive and personal qualities from its employees will it need to be successful?
* What can you contribute to the organisation as it journeys en route to achieving its vision?
* What are your long-term career goals – management, being a leader, being an entrepreneur? How hungry are you to achieve them?
* What does the consumer/client want? What are the trends and challenges facing the sector?

- What qualities will they be looking for in their employees? How can you show that you have them and, yet, that you can still add that extra something that's a bit different?
- What specific job skills does the recruiter call for, such as computing packages (word, excel, powerpoint, access and publisher)? What can you bring to the team that might be an added dimension?

Employers will also want soft skills, such as problem solving, communicating, teamwork, presentation, research, time management, meeting deadlines, and decision making. They'll want customer focus, ideas, solutions to problems and challenges, and energy, drive, ambition and hunger to get things done and done correctly. Can you show that you've brought ideas to the table before? That you've met targets, deadlines and kept your head and sense of humour and motivated others? Can you show that if they sponsor you for a professional qualification or a post-graduate course, that you'll commit to it in its entirety?

Each boss or line-manager has their own criteria to meet as they recruit for a role. These may refer to particular skills which are essential to the job – such as a language: 'Must speak fluent Russian' or 'Russian helpful'. They will be assessing every application throughout against these criteria and in fact they may ask the same questions of all candidates to compare their answers. There may be someone from human resources there to check any legal requirements, to ensure that the other interviewers remain on track and ask appropriate questions, and to cover company benefits. Your prospective boss will look at your skills set and how they will fit with his requirements and, crucially, how you will fit in with the team.

Personal fit with the team

There is not much you can do about this. You either fit, or you don't. And if you don't, it is nothing to do with you but more to do with the existing team as it is and the sort of person they want to add to it. For this reason, you may be called back for several interviews with different members of the team on each occasion to build up an all-round view of how you're going to fit in. View it each time as an opportunity to take a close look at your potential colleagues. What would it be like arriving for work every day first thing in the morning and making small talk by the coffee machine? It is essential to be yourself throughout the process if this fit is to be right, real and genuine.

Go into the recruitment process prepared to have fun

Most recruiters want to give you a good experience – they know you'll tell friends and family what you thought of them. They know that if you are not in a situation where you can be yourself, they're not going to get a glimpse of the true you, nor you of them. Many candidates are pleasantly surprised by the friendliness of those they meet at assessment centres, for example, be they fellow graduates or recruiters, and they often comment on how recruiters worked to put them at their ease. Of course, you'll always get the odd one who is not so friendly. The truth is that recruiters have a responsibility to take the right people on for the right roles, which is no easy task. And be prepared for the interviewer whose interview technique is appalling – rambling, non-stop, rude and arrogant. Visit the website www.doctorjob.com to read about graduates' experiences.

The assessment centre

Many (larger) companies use assessment centres to select their new recruits. These may last from a morning to a couple of days to see how you'll cope with the demands and stresses of the job with activities such as:

- ◆ Team tasks and activities;
- ◆ Knowledge test to find out how much you know about the area you propose to go into;
- ◆ Maths test to test your numerical skills;
- ◆ Written test;
- ◆ Test e.g. create a job advert or sift through CVs if you were applying to HR;
- ◆ Interviews;
- ◆ Presentations;
- ◆ Fitness test;
- ◆ Handwriting test;
- ◆ Medical;
- ◆ Tests specific to the company, such as their own driving test.

Consider the reasons why the organisation has included the tasks it has. Stand back and look quickly at the exercise from the employer's point of view. What competence or quality do you think they are looking for? Focus on each one as it appears. You may be asked to present on a subject unknown to you when you arrive so that the selectors can see how you handle presenting, debating and working under pressure. Think calmly and work out what you need to do. Maintain eye contact with your audience.

Social events may not 'count' towards your performance over the two days, but you'll certainly be quietly watched to see how you interact. Talk to the people you'll be working with and for. Find out what makes your potential work colleagues tick – will you want to be working with them every day of your working week under pressured circumstances? If offered alcohol, drink the absolute minimum you can. You want to be 110 per cent the next day while everyone else works at 80–90 per cent

Be yourself. It is exhausting to keep up any pretence over any period of time, and since both you and the company are trying to find out whether the two of you are suited to one another, it is also pointless. If you start off in an assessment centre and rapidly come to the conclusion that this company is not for you, then look at that as a positive. Hopefully the research you'll have done prior to applying for the job will prevent that happening. Have fun. Welcome the opportunity to test yourself, and be proud that you've got this far.

Attending an interview

Preparing for an interview or assessment day takes place at several levels:

* Researching the company;
* Reminding yourself of what you can contribute to that company and how it matches your career goals;
* Practical preparations, such as dressing the part, getting there with time to spare;
* Preparing mentally for questions you may be asked, such as What are your strengths? Tell us about a team effort you've contributed to and what your role was. Tell us about yourself!

- Preparing the night before – have an early night, keep alcohol to a minimum and don't eat anything with a strong flavour such as garlic;
- Getting yourself in the right frame of mind – there's no point in taking baggage that spells misery, depression, the 'Oh poor me, I'll never get a job' feeling. Leave it at home, put some music on which makes you feel really great en route, and focus on your positives.

A word about the 'Tell us about yourself' question. This is not an invitation for you to recite your entire life history. Outline in a couple of sentences where you are now and where you want to be. Keep it short and throw them a couple of points they can pick up on.

Interviews may form a part of an assessment centre process, or they may be held in their own right, especially if you're applying to small companies. Dress the part, as if you're applying for a job and not a date, so go for something slightly conservative. Before you attend an interview, check your image. Review your appearance head to toe and hand to hand. Is there anything you need to do, such as:

- Polishing shoes;
- Getting shoes re-heeled;
- Cleaning under your nails;
- Getting a hair cut;
- Improving the way you iron shirts or blouses;
- Making sure your suit isn't too tight;
- Checking the length of your skirt if you're a woman to make sure it's not too short;
- Looking to see what you could wear if you had to 'perform' two days running;
- Using accessories to boost your image without going over the top – a simple broach or tie-pin, for example;
- Not overdoing make-up, perfume or aftershave;
- De-cluttering your handbag, so that you can find items easily in it;
- Ensuring that your writing equipment – a pen and notebook – is easy to carry and appropriate (no pictures of cartoon characters or scribbles on the front), your pen works and you have a standby.

Take along a copy of your CV, a printed copy of any questions you have for the interviewers, and any research you've found on the company printed off the Internet. Take directions of how to get there, together with contact details of the person who organised the interview or who you're due to meet, in case you run into a problem en route. Charge your mobile. Account for any delays when planning your journey times.

Finally, review all you've learnt about the company, the sector you want to work in, the professional career you've chosen (if that's the case) and how your experience and skills will help the company to move forward and achieve its goals. Re-examine why you've made the decisions in your life that you have. Don't just rely on the Internet to research the company. If there is one of the company's stores or branches near you, go and visit it. Pick up information and brochures, or have them sent to you. Read them carefully and consider your visit: what impression did you have of the company and staff there? How comfortable would you feel having them as colleagues?

Do a final press search on the Internet; read the morning papers, eat a good breakfast, listen to music that makes you feel great, and head out to your interview. And remember – it's a two-way process and a chance for you to ensure that this employer is right for you, just as they need to make sure that you're right for them.

What sort of questions should you expect?

- Why us?
  Be positive about them and pick on two or three things which made them stand out against their competitors. It could be the clients they work with, their niche in the marketplace ...
- What did you think of ...e.g. our brochure, website?
  Once again, be positive and compare it against a couple of others you've seen in the sector.
- What do you think you'll be doing in the first year?
  Comment on the research you've done through talking with other graduates, and then embellish your answer by explaining that you do have a number of questions to ask them about the initial impact they expect you to make, progress in six months and five years' time.
- What is your perception of yourself?

This is all about how you think you present yourself to people. They may ask you how you think you present yourself to them.

+ What achievement are you proudest of?
  Think up several achievements before you go in and be prepared to talk about the work you put into making it so.
+ What salary are you expecting?
  Outline the research you've done in salaries in the sector, not just for new graduates but also more broadly speaking for others in the industry. Be prepared to negotiate and remember that the added perks can add up hugely. Consider your market worth before you go in; weigh up the amount of experience you've had and the strengths you have. If you're currently working, give your current salary.

Remember that good manners set you apart from other candidates throughout the process. No one wants to recruit someone who is rude, surly and sulky.

Handling weaknesses

Questions to ask the interviewers

Ask questions that will enable you to build up a picture of what sort of relationship you're likely to have with this employer and how your working day and week might look, both upon joining, six months after joining and then in about two to five years' time.

+ Is this a new position? If not, find out what happened to the previous or current post-holder. If the current post-holder is moving up or sideways, that's a signal of career progression (or a sideline move); if the post is new, find out the reasons why it's been created – you need to know you're heading for a new position that's been well thought through and is really needed.
+ Ask about the direction the company is taking – and how the company sees this post contributing to it.
+ Find out how long the interview process will take.

Table 7.2

Private healthcare	Joining bonus
Pension scheme	Personal accident insurance
Holidays	A sum of money to go towards a
Profit and performance related	course of the employee's choice
bonuses	Sharesave scheme
Buy or sell extra days holiday	Season ticket loan
Flexible working hours	Disability insurance
Child care discounts	Maternity and adoption phase-back
Discounted loans and mortgages	Summer shut down
Relocation packages	Company cars
Car lease schemes/discounts	Subsidised canteen
Financial support for professional	Language training
development	Sport and adventure training
Employee helpline	Insurance
Lifestyle managers	Travel cards
Pet insurance	Payment of professional association
Discretionary bonus	membership fees
Retirement plan	Work-wear
Social activities	

Offered the post!

Well done! Congratulations! Now, take a deep breath. Go some-where quiet to consider the options ahead of you. Is this offer really what you want? Will you be happy walking into the organisation every Monday? Can you fulfil your short- and longer-term career goals with it? Is the package right?

Add up perks and benefits

Perks vary, as employers provide increasingly individualised prod-ucts and services for their employees, and much depends on size and sector, but Table 7.2 shows examples.

Perks and benefits can all add up hugely. The question is: how is your salary likely to increase in the future? Bonuses will vary ac-cording to the industry you're in and how well your company – and/or you – perform. Find out what salaries are and what 'competitive' salaries in the industry are. Recruitment agencies and salary surveys will help you do just that. Look at the kind of positions you would expect to hold in, say, three or five years' time and see what the salaries and perks are for them. How different are they to what you currently earn?

Summary action points

Once you've started sending applications or taking steps towards your proposed first career move after your degree:

1   Keep a record of what you're sending out and when; this will help you to ascertain whether you're doing enough towards your goal.
2   Assess what is working particularly well and build on that.
3   Obtain feedback where you can to help you to improve your performance the next time.
4   Get involved in a couple of things in life other than careers and job hunting to help keep a balance in your day and week.

Chapter 8

What's stopping you?

Frequently in life, things seem to take far too long to go our way. We're waiting for that great job, or know that there isn't going to be one in the region we are in. We're waiting for a lucky break. But all too often, we are the people who stop ourselves getting what we want in life.

There are varying scenarios that we meet in life. For example, you can fall into a rut. You feel that you need a boost with the firepower of a space shuttle to get out of it, followed by a long sustained blast of persistent rocket fuel-type effort. This doesn't just happen in your career, but in relationships with people; perhaps the excitement has gone out of a relationship and you need a super-boost of impetus and excitement to bring it back to life. Perhaps your ability to be spontaneous in life has been overtaken by a preference for the known, safe and comfortable.

It may be that the situation you're in needs one bold, decisive step to get to where you want to be, but you feel like taking that step is like being asked to ski down the steepest, highest most icy slope. You just need to push yourself over the edge and set off, but it's making that first push which freezes you. At this point, we often fear failure and of looking like a fool in front of others – but we also fear success. We procrastinate from making that call, for fear of being turned down, rejected – but what if we succeed? How will we handle the changes in life that will invariably follow? Will we cope with them?

And then we make glorious plans, and life gets in the way. Family problems, a friend in trouble, illness, death, redundancy, changes thrust upon us, rows ... they all combine to be the reasons why we are where we are.

And sometimes, it seems that we aren't getting anywhere or at least where we want to be as quickly as we wish. Maybe we're waiting for that magic breakthrough – selected at interview, obtaining funding for that post-graduate course, securing an introduction and follow-up meeting with an employer you really want to work for, having a business idea while in the shower. We're waiting, confident that these things will happen one day. If we don't stay on top of things and create the right environment and conditions for success, we will probably wait a long time.

Don't forget what you went to university for!

If your career plans are taking an age to come to fruition, it can be really frustrating to see all those successful people at work who didn't go to university who say, *'Well, university wasn't for me, and now I'm a millionaire several times over'*. It can be easy to fall into the trap of blaming others for your current situation, thinking and saying things like *'Well, the school pushed us into it'*, and *'My parents thought it would be a good idea'*.

Five survival tips are:

1   Recognise that there are gifted people who chose not go to university but who have made it up the ladder by another route – people reach their potential in their own way and time; what matters is that they get there.
2   Keep everything in perspective – you have as much chance of succeeding as they do.
3   Learn from them.
4   Recall what you got out of your university days. No one can ever take them away from you, or your degree.
5   Focus on where you want to be. Review the progress you've made so far and assess how far you've moved towards achieving your main goals. Identify what else you need to do.

Dig deeper into your resources

Whether you fall into a rut or you need to take that one decisive step, there will always be stages in your life where you need to get tough with yourself and dig deeper within you for the resources you need to achieve the result you want: energy, focus, clarity of vision and action required, determination, an ability to go out there and get on with it. You've done it before, when you chose to apply to university, and then when you packed up and left home to head out there. It is *the* time to look afresh at the way you spend your time and energy and to get any unwanted stuff out of the way, such as anything that pulls you down.

Strengthen your resolve

You can choose to change your attitude, approach and luck, and you'll have subconsciously done so many times in your life when you felt good about what you were doing, things were going well, and you were on course for where you were heading. You may not have been aware that you were doing them. Since then, you probably picked up some bad habits, so it's a good time to make sure they aren't holding you back.

Dump the 'I'll try'. Trying isn't the answer

You can train yourself to think positively and talk positively by watching your language. If you're planning to do something, and think *'I'll try to do this before lunch tomorrow'*, then in fact you're unlikely to do it. Think *'I will do this tomorrow before lunch'*, and you inject a whole new energy into your focus and you're far more likely to get the thing done. Watch your language for a morning and listen for positive and negative statements. If you're talking more negatively than positively, that will be affecting your mood and manner. You can change that by simply talking more positively and changing your state and the way you're feeling.

What message are you taking on board?

Sometimes we don't help ourselves. If we're feeling down, and we watch a depressing television programme in which people are rowing and living mediocre lives, that's going to make us feel worse. If we listen to a piece of music we love and which makes us feel great and fantastic, then our approach to life changes.

Are you caught up in unhelpful patterns of thinking and behaviour?

Examples include criticising yourself, imposing limits or boundaries on the opportunities before you (such as thinking, 'Well, my indus-try is dead in this country. So what now?' instead of thinking, 'Where else is it functioning? How might it use my skills? Should I head out there for a holiday and see what's happening, or go into an allied industry?'). It involves giving yourself excuses for failing before you start, spending more time on socialising than job hunting, so not giving your career the prominence in your life that it deserves. Per-haps you're being too influenced by listening to generalisations from people who don't know what they're talking about; or you're not applying any creativity to your problem to find a solution.

Acknowledge there's a misunderstanding by others of what graduates can do for them

This is particularly the case in the SME market, where many bosses cannot keep up-to-date with all the changes in education at any level, unless they are parents. So make it easy for them. Pay particu-lar attention to your work experience when you write your CV and paint as clear a picture as you can for them of what you can do with clear examples. If you find a company that really excites you, why not find out whether there any initiatives in your area that will give you and the company support in making the most from each other? Regional Development Agencies in the UK would be a good place to start. Why not find out what small business networking groups are available in your area and offer to give a presentation of what life is like at university and the projects you've tackled along the way which help prepare you for work? What are universities doing to help small companies, and could that link provide a way in for you? The University of Nottingham for example has developed an SME Toolkit to help small companies overcome some of the issues they face in taking graduates on.

Use those problem-solving skills

What can you do to solve the problem?

1 Identify a problem you have now, such as finding that first right role, making your business work, or paying off your student debts.

2 Firstly, revise where you are now with the problem and identify the solution you want.

3 What is happening right now?
  + What are you doing which is working for you?
  + *You've tried everything?* Okay, ask yourself:
    + What exactly have you tried?
    + How often have you tried it?
    + When specifically?
    + How much time did you spend on it? How carefully did you do it?
    + Look back over the last seven days. What did you do on each of those seven days to tackle the problem? If you only spent an hour on Monday and Wednesday doing something, you cannot expect to solve it.

4 What extra resources and skills do you need to make the change happen? Table 8.1 below gives hints! Where will you get them from?

5 Look for new solutions.
  + Brainstorm every single thing you can think of that you might do to change the situation to make it just the way you want it to be.
  + What one thing do you need to do differently to get the results you need?
  + What else could you do?
  + What other ways could you approach the issue?
  + What would you advise a friend to do?
  + Who do you know who is where you want to be now?
  + What help and advice could they offer you?

Table 8.1

Extra	Contacts
Skills	Knowledge
Time	Experience
Energy	Influence
Qualifications	Materials
Opportunities	

- Who might have experienced the same problem before and could help you unblock where you are now by acting as a mentor to you?
  - If you're running your own company, what could you do to market yourself?
6   Finally, identify the actions you are prepared to take and when you're going to take them. Pinpoint any support you'll need and identify where you can get that from.

Focus on what you *can* change

Do something about the things you can change and don't waste time worrying about the things you cannot. When you look at the graduate recruitment market and your life after graduation, identify the things you can influence.

Pinpoint the missing angle which, once added, could lead to success

What do you need to do to turn your current position into a success and get to where you want to be? For example, you could consider:

1   Working for employers who naturally take on students with one or two years' experience after university. Why not find out how this route into the workplace would help you? Here your alumni associations with your old university could be invaluable.
2   Moving into an allied profession for a couple of years and then a change of track.
3   Relocating to where the opportunities are – which could be further afield than you like.
4   Working part time or on short-term stints until you find the right position. Go freelance!
5   Building up your skills through volunteering for charities and the public sector. Why not see if there is a project you could do for a charity close to your heart in your area or online?
6   Discussing your situation with relevant professional organisations; how flexible are the rules and regulations governing entry to and qualification for membership?

7 Starting your own business. There are lots of opportunities and programmes around for graduates who have business ideas, so find out what support and finance might be on offer and brainstorm that business idea!

8 Joining forces with fellow students from your course and brainstorming the issue together. What could you do collectively to turn the current situation into an opportunity?

Boost your creativity into solving problems and looking for opportunities. Get friends to help you brainstorm, and that way you're also tapping into their knowledge and creativity.

What practical steps can you take?

There could be *practical* steps you need to take to blow barriers away. Let's look at some of them.

Identify your skills gaps

Look at anything which may boost your employability, enhance your effectiveness and tackle your weaknesses, such as a public speaking course to improve your presentation style and confidence or learning new computer packages, which may be offered at a local further education college. In the meantime, what skills do you have which you could pass on to other people, such as students in school who need private tuition in a subject you've covered in depth at university? Are there any voluntary organisations in your area you could get involved with? It wouldn't pay, but it would mean you've done something extra to put on your CV, which would highlight your transferable skills, your ability to work with others and your initiative.

While waiting for a response ...

Keep sending out applications! You're probably doing this already but ask yourself what you can do differently with your applications which could make a difference next time and try to come up with as many creative ways as you can to source an opportunity.

One of the traps writers tend to fall into is that they will send out a proposal to a publisher or editor and then wait for a response. And while they're waiting, they do nothing. In fact, what they should be doing is congratulating themselves for getting a proposal out, and then heading straight back to their desks to work on the next one. So don't fall into the writer's trap; as soon as you've finished work on one application, start on the next.

How well are you promoting yourself?

From the minute you open your mouth, you're selling yourself. You need to show yourself as person who can be trusted. This goes with the CV but also in the way you handle people and situations. Basic social skills and good manners *are* important and a major complaint of employers and agencies right across the board is that they are sadly lacking in too many (younger) people today. Construct whole sentences, rather than using texting language that you'd send to your friends and family. Do not call people 'mate', 'darling' or any other form of endearment. They are not your 'mates'.

Some simple do's and don'ts now follow. Patronising? No, they are merely included because of employers' comments regarding the lack of basic social skills and manners in many graduates. Practice a warm firm handshake with your friends, looking people in the eye. Keep your shoulders back and square and your head up. You can practice this with strangers you meet in everyday life. When you meet new people, use this handshake and don't forget to accompany it with a smile. Drop the grunt; you're a graduate: sell yourself as such. Show yourself to be a positive, can do person. Leave the moods at home. We all get black days but there is no need to bring them to work. Do not whine about your current situation or blame past employers, teachers or anyone else for the state you are in. Be positive about going to university. You chose to do it and you gained from it, even though it may not seem like it right now.

Common concerns

I've just got a 2:2 ...
You're lucky. I've only got a third ...

Well, many employers are stipulating that yes, they do want a 2:1 or above and some are quite adamant that they won't consider anyone with lower than that. But there are plenty of good employers out there who *will,* and your task now is to focus not on what you cannot change but what you can do and influence to get your foot in the door. Focus on what you *can* offer in the way of key skills, personal qualities, drive and motivation – things you can promote and sell to an employer, who will want to know how you can contribute in the future. Could you work for that employer in a couple of years' time after getting some relevant experience behind you?

What about my age?

If you omit your age from your CV or application, employers will wonder even more about your age. Use your date of birth (not your age, e.g. 44 years) – it takes longer to work out so people are less likely to bother until later – and put it towards the end of your CV so that the recruiter can be excited about what you have to offer first. But, you know, there are good things too about being a mature worker and you should show that you mix easily with younger people (not mentioning children or grandchildren) in working situations, that you believe you can learn from each other, and get your image checked to make sure you look smart, crisp and fresh. Emphasise your work experience and the good points about maturity; many employers find mature staff more reliable. Show, too, that you can handle change well and that you're not stuck in your ways.

Being successful abroad

The key to success with a move abroad is to immerse yourself totally into the culture and to meet as many locals as you can. If you stick with people of your own nationality, you might as well have stayed at home. Learn a little of the language before you go, at least enough to be able to say some pleasantries; if you can, talk to people who've worked there so that you know what to expect and what the differences will be. Take pictures of your family and friends to show new friends that you're human too. Enrol in a language school when you arrive to boost your skills. Read the local papers to find out what's happening and observe local customs and, in particular, dress. Ultimately, you want to win people over rather than alienate them. Watch, listen and observe and see what you can learn from people.

Working abroad can offer you a wonderful opportunity to make a difference and get passionately involved in activities you love doing or want to learn – and you never know what will happen after that. You could meet your partner for life while working away which could totally change your long-term plans ....

Going down the self-employed route

Set yourself business and financial targets. Your bank or a business adviser can help you with this but you should have a clear idea of:

+ Your costs;
+ The equipment you'll need;
+ Drawings you'll take to pay yourself;
+ Any taxes and insurance;
+ The cost of taking on any employees;
+ What you propose to charge for your services;
+ How much of a profit you'll make on each item;
+ What the market is for it;
+ How you will market and promote your business and what the costs will be.

Many banks and building societies have specialist advisers working purely with franchise customers and the self-employed and you should look for one which falls into this bracket and who can give you lots of advice along the way. They may have specific products for the small business sector, partly in response to problems and challenges they face.

A word on family expectations

Family can particularly play a key role in our future career planning, unfortunately sometimes to the detriment of our own judgement of what is right for us. *'I went into it to please my parents'*, often means that graduates went into safe, respected careers which met with nods of approval and sighs of relief from their family, but made them, the graduate, feel they were en route to jail for a working lifetime. Today, most families are more relaxed about career choice – *'You can't tell them – they make their own minds up!'* frequently with all the inference that they still know better. They want us to be safe, protected, happy and successful, and a misunderstanding of the job market and a tendency to take on board negative messages from the media around us make things worse. There's nothing like the unknown and misunderstood to make people select the safe and known. While our friends and family have our interests very much at heart, their own agendas and self-interest may colour their well-meaning advice to us. They know our qualities well, but may have a limited experience and knowledge of the job market. Pinpoint ways to ask for their help. *'It would really help me if you could ...'* and suggest a couple of practical ways they could help.

If your family and friends have not gone through the process of higher education and have been in lower level jobs, seek to engage with people who are now in the career roles you aspire to, i.e. in the place where you want to be. Keep your sights high.

Access to finance

Apart from the obvious organisations to try, such as professional bodies and trade organisations, don't forget to tap into the various initiatives which may be taking part in your country or region to encourage growth and regeneration. Examples in the UK include the various industry cluster groups.

Find out what local business support groups have to offer

Pay a visit to your local BusinessLink's network and delve into the creative industries sector to see what's on offer in your area. In particular, firstly, they can help you to set up your own business, and secondly, they can help you to grow the business and give you help and information in areas such as exploiting your ideas, employing people, health and safety, premises, finance, grants and guidance on rules and regulations.

Learn from failure

If you're going to succeed in work, either as an entrepreneur or an employee, you need to be tough and tenacious, and to learn from failure. Two-thirds of all start ups fail in the first three years, for example, but many successful entrepreneurs point out that failure can be a tremendous learning tool. Failures give up their dreams and goals. They don't learn from the experience because they don't even try to see where they went wrong. They usually fall into the blame culture. Winners and successes may fail, but they learn from their failures and take the experience forward to build future successes.

Analyse failure, and you move forward. View it as part of the learning curve of life, and you'll come out much stronger for it. The tough times in life show you that you have what it takes to survive and come out of situations on top. As you get older, you realise how much you've grown from all those difficult times in work and personal lives. We all hit rough patches in life, like an aircraft going through turbulence, but we usually come out of it all the stronger for it. When you look back on something in this context, if you learn from an experience, you can hardly describe it as failure.

Don't take failure personally

If you didn't get that much cherished job you wanted, perhaps it simply wasn't meant to be – maybe someone else was simply a better fit for the post and the company. Take your 'failure' with you in the next interview and you won't win any friends. Invest in a punch bag or have a workout in the gym instead, obtain feedback if you can and review your performance yourself.

Ten survival steps for coping with failure

1   Have faith in yourself – there will be that perfect position for you somewhere out there, but you need to know what you're looking for. Keep focused and keep trying.
2   Keep knocking at doors. Get help and support around you, both experts in the field and your friends and family.
3   Ask for advice on turning those potential applications into sure bets.
4   Look for new strategies.
5   Keep a sense of perspective.
6   Don't turn to comfort eating, drink or drugs. It won't change anything. Keep healthy.
7   Learn from those who have failed but picked themselves up and gone on to be successful.
8   Obstacles in our way are often our unwillingness to say 'no' to people, or our belief in ourselves as much as anything real or physical.
9   Push yourself out of your boundary zone at every opportunity you get. You'll be surprised how much you can achieve.
10   Live life differently if you can. A fresh approach works wonders and avoids your getting stuck in a rut.

Summary action points

Identify barriers and obstacles and then do something about them through creative thinking.

1 Identify what barriers and obstacles you have ahead of you which may hinder you achieving your goals.
2 Now pinpoint as many ways to tackle them as you can.
3 Identify the one which will work best for you and do it.

Chapter 9

Moving on ... Your future

No matter who you work for, careers and businesses need nurturing and loving care just like any relationship in life. If you look after them, devote time and energy to them and focus on them, they will blossom. You need to give your career loving care, or it will degenerate into just a job.

First, though, you need to walk before you can run

So you've signed up, started work, and you know you're expected to hit the ground running and adjust to the workplace culture as quickly as you can. What can you do to make this easier for yourself?

Ask if you can go into the office and spend a couple of hours meeting colleagues before your official start date. This will give you a chance to find where things are (e.g. coffee machine, etc.) and get familiar with the area, so that you know where to get a sandwich for lunch, the nearest chemist, newsagent, etc. It will make the place seem less unfamiliar when you have that first day. Check the dress code (which you may or may not have had a chance to observe during the assessment process). If you're at all unsure, watch people leave the building and see how they are all dressed. Check your working hours, starting time for the first day, and whom you should report to. Work out what you're going to wear each day in that first week and make sure it's clean, pressed and that there are no buttons hanging off. Organise your meals for the week, so that you don't have to think about what to eat at night or buy food on the way home.

However nervous you are, be yourself and keep smiling. Most people recall what it was like on their first day; they will want to put you at ease. Remember that you need to put in a sustained effort, so don't burn yourself out by being over-enthusiastic and friendly in the first few hours. Ask for a buddy, someone who can help and guide you if you have questions about the place, someone you can turn to for advice and information. Talk to other staff at all levels in a friendly, interested way without overdoing it. They are human, after all, and you're hoping for a relatively long association with them as friends and colleagues.

As you meet people, a friendly firm handshake will do. Don't make this too firm and hearty, or give anyone a hug. Find out about the company policy regarding mobiles and personal emails; many firms review emails occasionally so watch what you write and who you send them to. Don't do blogs. Before you put any information online, consider carefully how it may be used. It could put future potential employers off you – how will they be able to trust you? And keep your own counsel; don't shoot your mouth off. Pick your confidantes and true work friends with care. Confidential means just that.

Starting work in any company can be frustrating for a few days or even weeks. You want to prove yourself, to do your best and to settle in. Yet being in a new work environment is just like being in a country you've never visited before, with lots to learn: how the computer system works, and whether there is an intranet; whose approval you need for what; who the key decision makers are; what the arrangements are vis-à-vis coffee and tea breaks/where you get them/whether you pay for them; and what people do at lunch time. You'll also learn who is who, what is where, and try to remember names and what people do.

Make an impact!

Seven ways to do this are:

1   Be friendly without being gushingly so. Don't call people 'mate'. They are not your mates (yet); they are work colleagues;

2   Listen and learn how things work before you dive in with comments; it can help to find out the history behind something which looks strange to you before you make suggestions;

3   Ask people questions about themselves and their role. *'What do you do? How long have you been here?'* It's a great way to make friends at work and learn who does what;
4   Be willing to stay late to get things done;
5   Double-check your work for accuracy;
6   Prove you're a safe pair of hands to be trusted and a team player who fits in. Take your turn getting the coffee, if that's what people do;
7   Be ready to begin at the bottom and use the opportunity to learn as much as you can about the way the organisation functions.

As well as working, there's the added stress of handling full-time work five days a week, and doing all those small but essential tasks needed to keep life ticking along smoothly. If you spend eight hours a day sleeping (56 hours a week) and nine hours a day working, including the commute to work, that leaves you with 67 hours a week to do your admin, banking and pay bills; laundry and ironing, cleaning and shopping, cooking, eating and washing up, personal hygiene and, more occasionally, check ups with the doctor, dentist, hygienist and gynaecologist, and taking the car to the garage for an MOT. You'll also want time to enjoy activities such as socialising, catching up with old mates, remembering your parents, leisure hobbies, exercise, having weekends away and that all important 'me' down time to relax and re-charge your batteries. On top of all that, you may have enrolled for further learning or work towards a professional qualification.

Studying for professional qualifications or a part-time post-graduate degree?

If you've decided to study for professional qualifications, talk to your current employer to find out what support they can give you. This may take a number of forms such as study leave or financial support, perhaps paying for all or part of the course, or your study materials or examinations. When approaching the subject, look to show how far the studies will boost your effectiveness on the job and benefit your employer, so that you present a 'win–win' situation.

Professional bodies should have information online regarding continued professional development, including which institutions are accredited to offer which course. Some have mentors who can help you with your time management and learning organisation, both essential ingredients to success.

Work out the time which is best for you to study. The time could be late at night, in the early hours of the morning or at the start of a new day. You know when you work best and at your most effective. It requires real motivation and dedication to do this. There will be many occasions when you just feel like switching off and doing something totally different or even nothing at all. Get advice from those who've been there before to learn from those who've done it. Find a quiet place and time to study and reward yourself afterwards. Above all, keep the reason you're studying for the qualifications at the forefront of your mind, because it will keep you going when times get tough.

It's not working out!

If you think things aren't going well as you try to settle into a new job, give it time. Ask for feedback on your performance and try to identify what it is that is not quite right. Perhaps time will help you settle or it could be that you need more support from your boss or line-manager. If that is not the case, view this role as a stepping stone to something better. It can take a couple of attempts to get the match of employer and role right; many employers appreciate that. In fact, some even deliberately take on graduates a couple of years after their degree, with the understanding that their first post may not have lived up to their expectations or worked out.

So what happens next?

There are a number of 'what' and 'where' and 'how' questions here. What have you achieved so far, and where do you see your career going next? Are there any potential barriers or obstacles which might hinder your progress and are there any extra resources you need to ensure success, such as skills or qualifications? Whether you are employed or self-employed, benchmark your progress and future plans against skills such as:

* Self-awareness
  Knowing your strengths, weaknesses, passions, ambitions, values and needs

* Self-promotion
  Raising your profile in the organisation and sector
* Exploring and creating opportunities
  Being proactive in taking responsibility for your own career development
* Decision making and action planning
  Making informed, decisive decisions that will take you in the right direction, and working out what needs to be done and when
* Coping with uncertainty
  Dealing with redundancy, restructuring, new clients, new tomorrows
* Transfer of skills
  Thinking laterally and broadly, applying the commonalities to the workplace and life
* Self-belief and confidence
  Yes, you can do it!
* Willingness to learn
  New products, new technology, new skills
* Commitment/dependability
  Everyone knowing you're a safe pair of hands, and management and your own staff trusting you
* Self-motivation
  Having drive and enthusiasm, and taking the initiative
* Co-operation
  People wanting to have you on board their team
* Communication skills
  Making yourself clearly understood in the right way and through various means
* Knowledgeable about new developments in the field
  Showing that you're up-to-date.

This benchmark will enable you to plot and plan your next steps effectively, pinpointing the learning and experiences you will need to get to the next stage. This is particularly important if you are in a lower level position than you had hoped for after leaving university or if you work for a small company. Set a long-term goal and break it down into manageable steps. Keep these at the forefront of your mind. While everyone else sleeps and parties, work at your goal. You'll soon climb the career ladder through your own dogged determination and persistence while they are left dozing or snoring their way through the working week.

Getting promoted

If you want to move up, plan for it so that you can prepare a path. For instance, if you get the chance to train any new staff or take responsibility for a group, do it; such an action will give your employer a chance to see how you put your management skills into action. Ensure your team knows what is expected of them and treat them all fairly and equally. When you delegate, check that people know what needs to be done, by when, and ask if they need any help. Explain why the task is important. Listen to their feedback and questions. Show how effective you are and tell your boss about the results you're getting.

Five ways to smooth the path to promotion

1   Make sure you have a regular review. If you aren't offered one, ask for one. Reviews will help you ascertain how you're progressing and where your career is heading in that organisation. They will help you check that you're on track to achieve your career goals in a time-scale which pleases you. Some companies review their staff every quarter, some every six months, others annually and many not at all.

2   Continually review the way you work – how can you handle your work-load more effectively and time efficiently while maintaining or improving your performance? Ensure you understand what your new role is about and what it contributes to the organisation's vision. Check that your team understands their mutual role, too – don't assume that they know – and make sure they are appropriately trained and motivated to achieve the results expected of them. As you progress up the ladder, working life and the accompanying rules will be slightly different, and you need to put a managerial hat on, rather than the technical, doing one you've had on before, and take a higher helicopter view. Delegate where you can, developing those you supervise through coaching, mentoring and one-to-one training. There are a number of excellent books on the subject, including Eric Parsloe's *The Manager as Coach and Mentor*.

3   Review your own performance every three months or so. Can you demonstrate the key attributes required to move to where you want to be? Do you need any extra skills to progress your

path, such as an MBA or a post-graduate or professional qualification? Are you getting stuck anywhere that you need help
with?

4   Dress for the role you aspire to, not the role you're in. Review
your wardrobe and image every six months. Always carry a
change of shirt/blouse and essential toiletries so that you can
refresh yourself prior to key meetings to give yourself an extra
confidence and energy.

5   *Network, network, network.* A strong network right across a
company could smooth your path into new roles and opportunities, and will raise your profile. It will strengthen your understanding of how different sections work and link together,
enhancing your performance: you'll know instantly who to
call for a piece of information, a contact or advice. Get on a
committee to get to know people and enable them to see how
you perform and interact with others. If you do something out
of the ordinary outside work, tell people about it. For example, if you've raised money for charity, write a short article for
your company newsletter. If you volunteer outside work for a
cause close to your heart, tell people. Or if you've done something slightly whacky at the weekend, write about that.

Are you working for a small company?

Sit down with the boss every six months or so to review your
progress and the results you have achieved. Then talk about your career progression. Look to build up your skills and experience – can
you take on more, for extra reward? Is there a project you can get
into which will give you a greater say? Look at how the company is
structured and who has the power and makes the decisions within
it. Is it something you would like to buy into in the future? If so,
what do you need to do to make that happen? Could the boss be
close to retirement and if so what would happen to the company
then? How would that affect you?

And outside the office ...

Networking is important as you move up the career ladder. Many
senior managers and professionals are recruited through recruitment agencies, head-hunters and search companies. These companies receive assignments from organisations which have roles to fill.

Headhunters will call around their contacts in the industry to see if they know of anyone who might fit the bill. Someone in your network may think of you ...

Make the most of your professional body

Many professional bodies have different types of membership depending on the stage you are at in your career. This means that there will be categories for students, graduates, young professionals, fully fledged professionals and sometimes, fellows, reserved for the most senior, experienced, qualified members of the body. Get involved in your region and give something back to those professionals coming through.

Continue to train and learn

You'll need to learn in and outside work throughout your life. A report called *Who Learns at Work?* produced by the Chartered Institute for Personnel and Development in the UK in 2005 shows that people do not take up training because they don't have enough time, or their family and personal commitments prevent them from doing so; others lack the motivation to do it, or their manager prevents it. View training as an investment, or an insurance, if you like, which boosts your employability.

As a graduate, you're more likely to ask for training because you are used to identifying your own training and learning needs and making sure they are met. Your university studies will have taught you how to learn through many methods, which will prepare you well for training at work. There are a huge number of ways to train, such as reading books and articles, taking correspondence courses, accessing learning materials on the internet and learning in a classroom or meeting room. You can also learn by being shown how to do things and then practising them, or through one-to-one training and coaching sessions with a manager or boss.

Consider learning a language

Employers are increasingly well aware of the benefits of having a workforce who can talk to customers and clients in their own language. In this small world, there is an increasing belief that senior executives need to be bilingual or multilingual to succeed in today's business world. It will become more important for executives to be at least bilingual and a significant competitive advantage for executives to be multilingual. If you can speak your customers' language, they will appreciate it, and working life is all about putting the customer's needs first.

What about an MBA?

If you're considering doing an MBA, contact the Association of MBAs (see Useful Addresses at the end of this book) which represents the international MBA community: its students, graduates, schools, businesses and employers. The Association promotes the MBA as a leading management qualification and aims to encourage management education at post-graduate level to create highly competent professional managers. MBAs benefit those students who want to be effective at a strategic level. There's plenty of opportunity to share ideas and experiences with students. The MBA provides an invaluable opportunity to develop your career, with a portfolio of managerial tools and techniques as well as the 'softer' skills needed to succeed as a manager such as an entrepreneurial spirit, dedication, commitment and professionalism. In some sectors, the MBA is a must have and it will help your chances of success, whether you decide to go on and work for someone else or to set up business on your own.

Leaving your current employer

The original contract between employer and employee has, for the most part, broken down. Employers are battling to be competitive, and the actions of restructuring and making employees redundant have impacted on their relationship with employees. Employees are ready to move if they don't get the career progression they want.

If you think you're coming to a dead-end in your current role, take stock of where you are. Perhaps your current role has run out of steam. Before you decide to leave, make sure that there are absolutely no other opportunities at your current company. Consider what you have done to create opportunities for expanding your role and taking on new projects and responsibilities. What is right with the job you have now? Often there's plenty we like about our work, and it's the bits we don't like that we tend to focus on and gripe about.

Now look forward. Have your ambitions got lost in the current role you're in? Before you decide whether you can achieve them with your current employer, talk to your boss and/or human resources and put an action plan together to help you get back on track. If your current employer cannot meet your future aspirations, *then* research a move to another organisation or setting up business on your own. Get the new deal signed before giving in your notice. Be discreet, and don't work at your CV in work time on a work PC. Use the Internet and specialist agencies, your network and company websites to help you find that next right move.

Attending interviews is trickier, because if you appear at work looking much smarter than usual and arriving late into the office, taking long lunch hours and leaving early, everyone will suspect you're job hunting. It may be worth simply investing the odd day's holiday here and there. And if you want to get work experience, because you want to go into something new, there are weekends, holidays and evenings.

Relocating abroad

If we choose to work abroad, many of us would like to think that we can go back to our homes after years away. Keep an eye on developments in your home country to make sure that time spent away doesn't prevent you from returning to your home country of birth, buying a house, settling down or anything else. When you're looking at any financial provision for your future, check to see what the taxation implications are if you move about. How will working abroad affect any pension due to you later in life, for example, be it state or private? A good accountant with international experience should be able to help you. Shop around to get the best deal you can.

So you've set up your own business and want to go for growth?

As you grow, delegate as much as you can, so that you're free to focus on the business. One possibility is to hire a virtual assistant, whom you would pay by the hour. Visit the website www.iava.org.uk to find out more.

Consider these questions:

- What have you achieved to date?
- What are your strengths, weaknesses, opportunities and threats?
- Where do you see yourself heading now?
- What extra resources do you need, e.g. time, money, equipment?
- Who can help you with that?
- What new products or services are you creating/innovating?
- What extra staff if any do you need and how will you find and employ them?
- What are you doing to build your niche and brand?
- What are your financial targets for the year?
- How much time are you devoting to business planning?
- What can you outsource, leaving yourself to focus on developing the business?

Look at the examples of perks listed earlier on page 111. Which are important to you long term and immediately? What do you need to do to make them happen? Many of them won't be critical, but you could incorporate them into your working life with a different slant. You could, for example, replace the opportunity to talk to an employee helpline with a monthly session with a coach or mentor. A loan from the bank may at least keep you watered, fed, sheltered and clothed. It is easy to put off thinking about retirement plans, but if you make a small contribution towards them now (the equivalent of ten pints of beer a month, for example), your spending and savings habits will be established for life.

Finally, you may be working in the day to get some money coming in and tackling your 'real' job at night, hoping to resign when you hit a breakthrough. If this sounds like you, make sure your 'night' job is honestly going places by asking the following questions:

What have you achieved overall so far?

- What is working well?
- What marketing is going well?
- Where can you create more time in your day?
- Where do you want to be in six months' time?
- What will you need to do to make that happen?
- Who can help you further?

♦ What do you need to do to move your business to the next stage?

Flexibility and adaptability go a long way to making the most of life

You may be merrily making your way through your career and then something happens which changes everything for you at a stroke.

Ten events which could change your life and your career

1   You meet your future partner; and life is never the same;
2   Your create a baby and parenthood is on the way;
3   You hit on a business or social idea which, if implemented, will really make a difference;
4   You or one of your relatives or a friend falls seriously ill or has an accident and needs special care and love; plus it makes you re-think;
5   You get head-hunted;
6   A major world event makes you rethink life;
7   You volunteer for a cause you believe in;
8   You decide to live abroad;
9   You win the lottery;
10 You take the decision that you want to live a higher quality life and set about doing just that.

Summary action points

Take responsibility for enhancing your own employability:

1   Keep a track of any ways in which recruitment methods for your sector change.
2   Who are the key players in the market you're in for recruitment? Who are the main agencies?
3   Don't stay with an employer if they're not enabling you to meet your career goals. Do what you can to ensure that the doors to your advancement are truly shut – and then leave. You could be surprised.

Chapter 10

Here's to life!

Take a holistic view of your life and health and happiness are more likely to be yours.

Take a narrow, focused view of it, concentrating on only one aspect, and the other areas will suffer. There will be times when one aspect of your life – such as your career – takes priority over others. But that doesn't mean that the rest of your life should lose out totally. If you're not fit and healthy for example, it will be harder to maintain a peak performance at work – which could make all the difference to whether you get that promotion or make that next step or not. Continually look at your life to consider questions such as:

- What do you want in your life besides your career?
- What are you doing to enjoy life?
- What are you doing to pay off your loans?
- What are you doing to start building financial security for yourself?

We just have one life, so make time for those things which matter to you most, such as family, friends and fun. The way you manage your resources – time, energy, money, health and relationships – can make a huge difference to the quality of life you enjoy.

What are the things you want in your life to be happy and fulfilled? Do any of the examples in Table 10.1 feature?

From the day we are born, life often gets in the way, throwing trials, tribulations and challenges at us. Working towards some 'wants' and 'must haves' in your life may demand that you 'park' other things aside for several weeks or months while you focus on them or a project that is of particular importance to you – such as your wedding day or training for a marathon. But a balance helps keep things

Table 10.1

Family – perhaps children	Key relationships and roles
Pets	Fun and laughter
Friends	Volunteering
Travel	Cultural and leisure activities
Dreams	Nature
Adventure	Excitement
Material goods	A good sex life
Achievements	Nice place to live
Financial assets	Solid retirement plans
Health and vitality	Great memories
Spirituality	Other

in perspective. And the work–life balance becomes a hot topic as individuals struggle to find ways to cope with the demands of work and personal commitments to family and friends. Balance is important in many aspects of life and Table 10.2 below gives suggestions as to where this balance is important.

How balanced is *your* life?

Every year, check your work–life balance is as you want. Assess how content you are with each area of your life which is important to you and to pinpoint those which need work and which you want to change. The Wheel of Life exercise in Figure 10.1 below allows you to do just that.

Each segment in the wheel represents an area in your life which you identified earlier in the chapter as being important to you. So:

1   From the categories you ticked in Table 10.1, allocate a segment to them.

Table 10.2

Work	and	Leisure
Work	and	Holidays
Rest	and	Exercise
Healthy food	and	A bit of what you fancy
Smooth running of life	and	Challenges
Certainty	and	Uncertainty

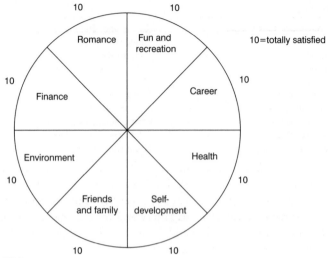

Figure 10.1

2   How satisfied are you right now with each one? Rate them in-
     dividually from 0 to 10. Totally satisfied earns a 10; complete
     dissatisfaction at the centre a 0.
3   Draw a line or curve in each segment to represent how satis-
     fied you feel with your life at the moment.

  How does your life look? How many segments are a 10?

1   Which segments need working on (i.e. are below a 7)? What
     would they have to be like for you to rank them as a 10?
2   What do you need to do to make that happen?
3   What will you do to make them happen and when?

   Of course, you could take one segment of the wheel and make a
wheel of it in its own right. Thus you could have a Career Wheel,
with segments on growth, learning, responsibilities, rewards, skills
and interest. You can keep changing the wheel from one month to
the next as you work to improve each sector.

But work's taken over my life!

More employees are now finding that short breaks recharge their
batteries quite adequately without a huge panic about sorting out

the in-tray before and after a longer break. A good proportion put off their holidays and don't take the full allowance, *'I'm too busy at work'*. Very few of us can keep going at premium performance without having some sort of regular break built into the day. Our own bodies have their own needs; one person may be able to do with very little sleep, while others need a lot. If you don't listen to your body, sooner or later it will pay you back when you least need it, to remind you that it has needs too, such as *proper* rest and recuperation. You're not indispensable. It's sad to say, but if you were killed by a bus today, your company *would* go on without you. If you don't look after yourself, you are unlikely to be able to look after others.

There are some careers in which long hours are the norm, but it can be easy to fall into the trap of doing long hours for the sake of it. The person who never takes a lunch break can rarely work at the same performance level throughout the day. The person who always takes a break away from the phone, email and work environment can only find her performance enhanced. No excuses! Walk around the block for 20 minutes and boost your heart beat, reduce your stress levels, keep that weight down *and* boost your mood.

Stress

With all the hype about stress, remember that the right sort of stress can help you live longer. Mild to moderate stress increases the production of brain cells, enabling them to function at peak capacity, so if you want to live life to a peak performance, get stressed but in the right way – it makes your body and mind stronger.

Beneficial stress gives you recovery time and a sense of accomplishment afterwards. It challenges you, although you may complain about it at the time. The bad stuff is sustained and unrewarding. You need to find the middle ground somewhere between the two and build it into your daily life. Look for activities which reward and stimulate you, such as a run before work, studying in the evenings or voluntary work at weekends.

Get out of your comfort zone and take part in something which isn't routine and predictable or effortless. The more you look for these sorts of activities, the more you'll benefit. Collapsing in front of the TV after a day's work with a glass of wine isn't beneficial. Playing some sort of sport or going to adult education is. It's important to face stress or challenges mentally, physically, socially and spiritually. Don't waste time dwelling on the problems and demands of life – think about the pleasure, variety and vigour that challenges bring us and you'll feel much more alert and in control. Many challenges arrive through the roles we choose to play in life.

What roles do you want to play?

We all have roles in life and they all tend to appear at different times. Table 10.3 shows roles most of us experience in our lives.

Our roles and relationships and the responsibilities that come with them intertwine with careers more than any other aspect of life. Which comes first: career or ageing relative? The presentation or a sick child? The school play or your squash game? The carer in us may play a key role and take centre stage in our lives while our parents get older and need decisions to be made for them. The parent has a lifelong role, but spends more time on it in the early years of a child's life and that role changes as life progresses, such that their children become their friends in adulthood. Our relationships with our siblings change, too, particularly as we all settle down into adult life and face the challenges of dealing with ageing parents.

Our friends, too, change. We keep some throughout life; others we see enter at different stages and then leave, as if they came for a reason. Perhaps they were there to teach us something, to make us laugh at a time when we felt low, to make us feel good about

Table 10.3

Parent	Friend
Son/daughter	Volunteer
Manager	Leader
Supervisor	Confidante
Doer	Thinker
Teacher	Adviser
Loner	Niece/nephew
Aunt/uncle	Grandparent
Actor	Diplomat
Neighbour	Carer
Sister/brother	Cousin
Good Samaritan	Hero

ourselves, or just ... because. We need friends, both on our own account and when with a partner. Friends help you to keep things in perspective. A true friend is there for the good and bad times and will see you through.

If we're to have successful, empowering relationships, we need to put boundaries on what we will and won't do in our role. We may tire of the friend who calls us just once too often in the early hours of the morning, distraught over a break-up. We may be fed up of being the only sibling who makes an effort with our parents, while our siblings bleat that they are 'too busy'. Assertiveness is important if friendships and relationships are to thrive and grow. Saying 'no' is important in any role, if we are to feel strong and right. Saying 'yes' to keep the peace usually leads to feelings of resentment and disappointment in ourselves for not having the courage to say what we really want to say. Saying 'no' is a sign that we feel confident enough in ourselves to say what we mean and, crucially, that we care about ourselves and what we undertake in life.

Develop your ability to handle people

1   Identify your boundaries in any relationship – the rules you feel comfortable with and stick to them.
2   Look at things from the other person's point of view. Put yourself in their shoes to get an idea for how they are feeling.
3   Remember that you cannot change other people – but you certainly *can* change the way you behave towards them.
4   Work on what you know you *can* influence, as opposed to the things you cannot.

Use your resources effectively

We have a tremendous amount of resources at our disposal, from mind-mapping to help creativity, speed reading to enable us to acquire knowledge more quickly, our memory to help retain it, meditation to help us focus and exercise to boost our energy. But the thing most people want more of today is time.

Is your time management letting you down?

'I haven't got time', is a common complaint. And yet how often do you reassess the way in which you spend your time (and money)?

- Track the ways in which you spend your time;
- Look back at your wheel of life and the activities you identified as important to you;
- How much of the 168 hours a week do you spend on them?
- Decide what to do about any imbalance?

If you learn from this exercise that you're only spending two hours a week making new friends, but that friendship is important to you, then something in your week needs to change. You may need to sacrifice something else to allow room for the change to happen. If you want to work on your portfolio but only devote three hours to it, and four evenings to going out with friends, although your social life is going to look pretty good, your portfolio won't. Devote four evenings to your portfolio, and that fifth evening spent with friends really will feel well deserved.

Track the way you spend your time for a week. In particular, track the time you're wasting on any of the activities in Table 10.4.

Identify the three which waste most time for you and how much time they take up. What difference would it make if you didn't spend time on them? What are you going to do to get rid of them and what will you do with your time instead?

Undertake exercises like this while you're still at university, when you've graduated and later on when you have work, family and house maintenance responsibilities, when you are commuting and studying for professional qualifications, and have social and leisure activities to fit in. You can also apply it to your working day to find out how you can use your time more effectively at work.

Table 10.4

Negative people/thoughts	Missing deadlines
Unanswered messages	Difficulty communicating
Outstanding letters and bills	Computer illiterate
Lacking confidence	Non-assertiveness
Unnecessary texting/emailing	Information overload
Losing things, e.g. keys	Smoking
Surfing the Internet	Drink and drugs
Broken items	Gambling
Too much TV	Fears
Poor sleep	Anxieties
Flitting from one thing to another without any real focus	Doubts
	Unnecessary meetings

Do the same exercise with money

- ◆ What financial base do you want to build up in the future?
- ◆ What do you need to do to make that happen?
- ◆ What is getting in the way?

Identify the financial resources you want and then you can start making them happen. Some items are essentials, such as a property to rent or buy, living costs and tax and state demands, e.g. national insurance. After that, saving is usually a wise move for that rainy day, and so is insurance. There are also a whole range of investments, savings accounts, stocks and shares which are best discussed with a financial adviser.

Ten ways to review your finances continually

1 Where is your money going?
2 Which items are essential, important, nice to have?
3 Where can you cut back?
4 What will do to make that happen?
5 Which items do you no longer need and could sell?
6 How could you make more money? Examples include focusing on career development so that your salary increases.
7 Who can help you sort out your debts and finances?
8 What do banks and building societies offer graduates?
9 What realistically can you achieve in the next week, six months and three to five years? How can you capitalise on that? Put any unexpected windfalls such as a bonus or present into paying off your loan straight away.
10 How rigorously are you making your money work for you?

Make your money work for you. Be proactive in looking for the best deal, the highest interest rates which suit your needs, the lowest loan rates, and keep looking. Do a three-monthly financial MOT and reward yourself for your financial acumen. The higher you climb the career ladder, the greater the perks and salary. Working for professional qualifications at night will not only boost your employability but also keep you away from expensive bars and nightclubs, keep your money in your pocket and enable you to pay off your loans and debts faster.

Most people continually believe they are short of time and money, but don't proactively do enough specifically about it. It takes discipline, effort and creative thinking to sort out your finances. Paying off a loan doesn't take forever, even though it may seem like it. Much depends on *how* focused you are in paying off your loans. And if you nurture your career, your financial status should get better as you're rewarded for your efforts. Careers take up around 48 weeks a year out of 52 and subsequently impact on your overall quality of life, so surely they are worth the effort and dedication?

Living at home with your parents after university

Many young people are moving back home after university to save money, to pay off debts and for an assortment of other reasons. But what other options do you have apart from moving back in with your parent(s)? Could you get in touch with other graduates in the area or on the same graduate trainee scheme in your company who are in the same boat and flat-share, or live abroad in a country where graduates are welcomed and it is easier to get on the housing ladder? If you still decide to return home (perhaps you never left), work out a financial arrangement so that you pay your parent(s) rent (even if it is a very small amount) – you need to keep in the habit of budgeting for your housing. And arrange with them what your contribution will be towards the house-keeping, be it cleaning, washing, helping in the garden, cooking a meal a couple of times a week. Don't fall back into the ways of a teenager having everything done for you. You've moved on from that and so have your parents, so don't use your parents' home: sit up, take some responsibility and *contribute* to it. Sit down and agree a few house rules (just as you would have had at university with your flat mates) to keep everyone happy and remember to practice the art of negotiation and compromise. Finally, consider these questions:

+ How long do you intend to stay with your parents? Give yourself a deadline to leave and stick to it. Do you want to be living with them when you're 40?
+ How much of your student debt will you have paid off by that time? How will you do it?

• What will you have achieved in your career by then and how will that have boosted your income to help you start building a financial base?

Finally, when the time does come to move out, why not get your parents a small gift as a token of appreciation for their help over the years? Parents are usually very happy to help out their offspring – but it is always nice to be appreciated and thanked.

Don't forget the wild and wacky

What would your life be like if you drew up a list of all the things you wanted to do and achieved before your eightieth birthday? What a glorious blaze of memories you could have to look back on as your older years set in!

List the things you want to do and the reasons *not* to do them will fade into the background. You'll be filled with a tremendous energy and enthusiasm, passion and excitement as you start identifying how and when you're going to do it all. Writing your list down enhances your determination to make your items happen. Keep your list where you can easily see it *frequently*. Show your list to those who are important to you in your life. Suggest they draw up a list of their own, and compare notes. Are there things you can do together? Can you give each other the time and space required to make them happen? You need to make sure that those you love don't constrain you in a plant pot, so that your roots can't spread out and grow. If they do limit you, it may be time to say farewell to the relationship. A rich relationship should enable you to take some journeys as a couple and others alone.

Don't become a robot

It's easy to fall into a continuous cycle of work, supper, TV, bed. The more you do, the more you'll want to do and the dream list above can help you do just that! And as you push back your boundaries outside work, it will also become much easier to do just that in your working life. At the start of this book, you identified what success and happiness meant to you. Perhaps you listed things like a large bank account, exotic holidays, happy, healthy kids who stay off drugs and alcohol; giving something back to the community which really makes a difference, a particular status in the community or organisation.

You need to decide how important success is to you and in what capacity. Occasionally, you may tweak or transform your ideas of success and happiness or completely change them. But in the hustle, bustle and noise of life, take time out to dream and look into the present and future to ensure you're spending your life on activities which, and with people who, are important to you. Get focused and create the life and success you want.

Looking forward

The goal posts of life are for your own positioning. Be clear about the things you want to change in your life and what you want out of it, and then take personal responsibility to make it happen. You may need to work around barriers and obstacles, regulations and rules along the way, but that makes the end achievement all the more rewarding.

Your degree over, you have a chance to look back, contemplate, reflect and congratulate yourself, and to look forward, to plan and build your future. Pause to do this at regular intervals in your life and it will feature the activities and achievements which are important to you.

Finally, consider what really is important in life. Do any of these elements feature for you?

1   Love and be loved;
2   Be passionate about a cause;
3   Wonder at the beauty of the earth and nature's sheer power;
4   Feel at peace;
5   Laugh and see the funny side;
6   Care for those you know and those you don't;
7   Be curious: don't lose the habit of asking what, why, when, where, who, how;
8   Learn from those who've gone before you and who'll come after you;
9   Use your creativity and imagination to the full;
10 Create you own luck, success and happiness.

And remember:

Nobody ever said: 'I wish I'd spent more time at the office' on their deathbed.

Summary action points

Your life
Your future
Your choice
Good luck!

Chapter

Further reading

Careers related

Alexander, L. (2003) *Turn Redundancy to Opportunity*, Oxford: How To Books Ltd.

Barrett, J. and Williams, G. (2003) *Test Your Own Aptitude*, London: Kogan Page Ltd.

Brown, C. (2005) *Working in the Voluntary Sector*, Oxford: How To Books Ltd.

Lees, J. (2005) *How to Get a Job You'll Love*, London: McGraw-Hill.

Williams, N. (2004), *The Work We Were Born to Do*, London: Element Books Ltd.

Business and finance related

Forsyth, P. (2001) *Getting a Top Job in Marketing*, London, Kogan Page Ltd.

Forsyth, P. (2002) *Getting a Top Job in Sales and Business Development*, London: Kogan Page Ltd.

Longson, S. (2002) *Getting a Top Job as a Personal Assistant*, London: Kogan Page Ltd.

Stanley, A. (2003) *Careers in Marketing, Advertising, and Public Relations*, London: Kogan Page Ltd.

Prospects (www.prospects.ac.uk) has 400-plus occupation profiles.

See also these AGCAS booklets and DVDs (www.agcas.org.uk) on subjects such as

- City markets;
- financial services;
- legal;
- professional services;
- advertising and PR;
- tourism.

Recruitment

See the website www.alec.co.uk for lots of formats and examples of CVs.

Bishop-Firth, R. (2004) *CVs for High Flyers*, Oxford: How To Books Ltd.

Bryon, M. (2005) *Graduate Psychometric Test Workbook*, London: Kogan Page Ltd.

Johnstone, J. (2005) *Pass that Interview: Your Systematic Guide to Coming Out On Top*, Oxford: How To Books Ltd.

Yate, M.J. (2002) *The Ultimate CV Book*, London: Kogan Page Ltd.

Yate, M.J. (2003) *The Ultimate Job Search Letters Page*, London: Kogan Page Ltd.

Yate, M.J. (2005) *Great Answers to Tough Interview Questions*, London: Kogan Page Ltd.

Moving up the career ladder

Bishop-Firth, R. (2004) *The Ultimate CV for Managers and Professionals*, Oxford: How To Books Ltd.

Hughes, V. (2004) *Becoming a Director*, Oxford: How To Books Ltd.

Purkiss, J. and Edlmair, B. (2005) *How To Be Headhunted*, Oxford: How To Books Ltd.

Shavick, A. (2005) *Management Level Psychometric and Assessment Tests*, Oxford: How To Books Ltd.

Working abroad

Carte, P. and Fox, C. (2004) *Bridging the Culture Gap: A Practical Guide to International Business Communication*, London: Kogan Page Ltd.

Doing Business With, an excellent series published by Kogan Page Ltd covering these countries: Bahrain, Croatia, Saudi Arabia, UAE, China, Jordon, Kazakhstan, Kuwait, Lybia, Serbia and Montenegro and the EU Accession States.

Going to Live in ...and *Living and Working in* ...two highly informative and practical series published by How To Books Ltd (Oxford), covering countries such as Spain, Australia, New Zealand, France, Italy and Greece.

Khan-Panni, P. and Swallow, D. (2003) *Communicating Across Cultures*, Oxford: How To Books Ltd.

Reuvid, J. (2006) *Working Abroad: The Complete Guide to Overseas Employment*, London: Kogan Page Ltd.

Vacation Work Abroad have a plethora of publications which give you ideas on how you can work your way around the world.

Self-employment

Blackwell, E. (2004) *How to Prepare a Business Plan*, London: Kogan Page Ltd.

Bridge, R. (2004) *How I Made It: 40 Entrepreneurs Reveal All*, London: Kogan Page Ltd.

Gray, D. (2004) *Start and Run a Profitable Consultancy Business*, London: Kogan Page Ltd.

Isaacs, B. (2004) *Work For Yourself and Reap the Rewards*, Oxford: How To Books Ltd.

Jolly, A. (2005) *From Idea to Profit*, London: Kogan Page Ltd.

Power, P. (2005) *The Kitchen Table Entrepreneur*, Oxford: How To Books Ltd. Turn that hobby into a profitable business!

Reuvid, J. (2006) *Start Up and Run Your Own Business*, London: Kogan Page Ltd.

Stone, P. (2002) *The Ultimate Business Plan*, Oxford: How To Books Ltd.

Whiteley, J. (2003) *Going for Self-Employment*, Oxford: How To Books Ltd.

Gap year/time out

Potter, R. (2004) *Worldwide Volunteering*, Oxford: How To Books Ltd.

Vandome, N. (2005) *Planning Your Gap Year*, Oxford: How To Books Ltd.

Further study

Marshall, S. and Green, N. (2004) *Your PhD Companion*, Oxford: How To Books Ltd. Contains a great selection of tips and advice to help you through your PhD.

Career and life success

Drummond, N. (2005) *The Spirit of Success*, London: Hodder and Stoughton.

Ebury, S. (2003) *Moving On Up*, London: Ebury Press.

Hill, N. (1996) *Think and Grow Rich*, New York: Ballantine Books. Robbins, A. (1991) *Awaken the Giant Within*, New York: Simon and Schuster.

Tracy, B. (2003) *Goals! How to Get Everything You Want – Faster than You Ever Thought Possible*, San Francisco: Berrett-Koehler Publishers Inc.

Learning skills

Bradbury, A. (2006) *Successful Presentation Skills*, London: Kogan Page Ltd.

Claston, G. and Lucas, B. (2004) *Be Creative*, London: BBC Books Ltd.

Covey, S. (2005) *The 7 Habits of Highly Effective People: Powerful Lessons in Personal Change*, London: Simon & Schuster UK Ltd.

Lilley, R. (2006) *Dealing with Difficult People*, London, Kogan Page Ltd.

Parsloe, E. (1999) *The Manager as Coach and Mentor*, London, CIPD.

Wiseman, Dr R. (2004) *The Luck Factor: Change Your Luck – and Change Your Life*, Sydney: Random House Australia (Pty) Ltd.

Managing others

Charney, C. (2001) *Your Instant Adviser: The A–Z of Getting Ahead in the Workplace*, London: Kogan Page Ltd.

Morris, M.J. (2005) *The First-Time Manager: The First Steps to a Brilliant Management Career*, London: Kogan Page Ltd.

Taylor, D. (2005) *The Naked Leader*, London: Bantam Books.

Whitmore, J. (2002) *Coaching for Performance*, London: Nicholas Brealey Publishing.

Building financial bases

Ahuja, A. (2004) *The First Time Buyer's Guide*, Oxford: How To Books Ltd.

Bowley, G. (2005) *Making Your Own Will*, Oxford: How To Books Ltd.

Chesworth, N. (2004) *The Complete Guide to Buying and Renting Your First Home*, London: Kogan Page Ltd.

Palmer, T. (2005) *Getting Out of Debt and Staying Out*, Oxford: How To Books Ltd.

Life related

Fortgang, L.B. (2002) *Take Yourself to the Top*, London: Thorsons.

Gaskell, C. (2000) *Transform Your Life – 10 Steps to Real Results*, London: Thorsons.

Useful addresses and further information

General

Association of Graduate Careers Advisory Services
Administration Office
Millennium House
30 Junction Road
Sheffield S11 8XB
Tel: 0114 251 5750
www.agcas.org.uk

Hobsons
www.hobsons.com
A website with lots of features to help you get that right job wherever you are

Prospects
www.prospects.ac.uk
A huge source of information and useful links for graduates of every discipline

Inside Careers
www.insidecareers.co.uk
Information on accountancy, banking, IT, logistics, management consultancy, tax and more!

UK regional graduate websites

Many of the sites below are designed to help graduates returning to the region or wishing to move to the area:
Yorkshire and Humber Region: www.graduatelink.com
Graduates Yorkshire: www.graduatesyorkshire.info

Graduates North East: www.graduates.northeast.ac.uk
Merseyside-Business Bridge: www.business-bridge.org.uk
Merseyside: www.gieu.co.uk
Merseyside Workplace: www.merseyworkplace.com/
North West Student and Graduate On-Line: www.nwsago.co.uk
North Midlands and Cheshire Employers Directory: www.soc.
staffs.ac.uk/eh1/emp2003.html
Staffordshire Graduate Link: www.staffsgradlink.co.uk
Graduate Advantage: West Midlands: www.graduateadvantage.
co.uk
Gradsouthwest.com: www.gradsouthwest.com
GradsEast: www.gradseast.org.uk
The Careers Group, University of London: www.careers.lon.ac.uk
Graduate Ireland: www.gradireland.com
Scotland Graduate Careers, managed by Services to Graduates
Group: www.graduatecareers-scotland.org
Scotland – Graduates for Growth: www.graduatesforgrowth.co.uk
GO Wales: www.gowales.co.uk

Work experience and initiatives, and voluntary work

Knowledge Transfer Partnership
www.ktponline.org.uk/graduates

National Council for Work Experience
Tel: 0845 601 5510
www.work-experience.org
enquiries@work-experience.org

www.do-it.org
Find out what opportunities there are to volunteer in the region
you live in

Many also provide work placements such as:

Graduate Business Partnership
scheme run by the University of Exeter
www.ex.ac.uk/businessprojects

Merseyside-Business Bridge
www.business-bridge.org.uk

Merseyside: www.gieu.co.uk.
A programme of events to enhance your employability and prepare you for a competitive job market with representatives from various sectors

GO Wales
www.gowales.co.uk

West Midlands Graduate Advantage
www.graduateadvantage.co.uk

Further study

Association of MBAs
25 Hosier Lane
London EC1A 9LQ
Tel: 0207 246 2686
www.mbaworld.com
Has a full list of accredited MBA courses, plus links to institutions, and details of the MBA fair, scholarships, awards loans. The Official MBA Handbook can be acquired over their site and gives you all the information you need to get started. There's also information about rankings

British Council
10 Spring Gardens
London SW1A 2BN
Tel: 0161 957 775
www.britcoun.org
The British Council has a network of offices throughout the UK and in 110 countries worldwide. Visit its website or one of its offices for more information on funding, scholarships and studying in the UK. You will also find a lot of information about Arts, Science and Society in the UK

E-learning foundation
www.e-learningfoundation.com

ww..direct.gov.uk
Information on adult learning, including funding, learning through voluntary work and e-learning.

National Post-Graduate Committee
www.npc.org.uk
The NCP represents the interests of post-graduate students in the
UK. Information on funding, discussion boards, post-graduate facts
and issues, and post-graduate careers. Also an academic job search
with international links to jobs in the USA, Canada and Australia
amongst others

UKNARIC
Oriel House
Oriel Road
Cheltenham
Gloucestershire GL50 1XP
Tel: 0870 990 4088
The National Recognition Centre for the UK and National Agency
for the Department for Education and Skills
www.naric.org.uk
The only official information provider on the comparability of
international qualifications from over 180 countries

Ploteus
www.europa.eu.int/ploteus
The European course search portal

Post-graduate study and research

www.research-councils.ac.uk
A partnership set up to promote science, engineering and technology supported by the eight UK Research Councils. Grants are
allocated to individual researchers, networks of people working on
projects, programmes, designated research centres, fellowships and
post-graduate students
Higher Education and Research Opportunities in the United
Kingdom

www.hero.ac.uk
Has an excellent section on research with links to the main
research councils, universities and others, plus information on how
to disclose your findings as a new researcher

The Royal Society
www.royalsoc.ac.uk

British Academy
www.britac.ac.uk

British Council
www.britcoun.org.uk

National Union of Students
www.nusonline.org.uk

The United Kingdom Research Office (UKRO)
www.ukro.ac.uk
An information and advice service on EU funding for research and higher education

Universities UK
www.universitiesuk.ac.uk

www.findaphd.com
This website is the largest directory of PhD opportunities in the UK

Self-employment

British Franchise Association
Thames View
Newton Road
Henley-on-Thames
Oxon RH9 1HG
Tel: 01491 578 050
www.thebfa.org
For information on franchises, both in and outside the UK, finding a franchise, successful case studies and events, a list of members. Ask for a copy of the British Franchise Association Franchisee Information Pack and check when the next Franchise Exhibition is near you on its website

BusinessLink
www.businesslink.gov.uk
A network of business advice centres in England with allied bodies in Scotland, Wales and Northern Ireland, all accessible through this site

Prime Initiative
Astral House
1268 London Road
London SW16 4ER
Tel: 0208 765 7833
www.primeinitiative.org.uk/
Dedicated to helping those over 50 to set up their own business

Prince's Trust
Tel: 0800 842 842
www.princes-trust.org.uk
Help for the 14–30 year old who wants to set up his or her own business or tackle barriers to employment

Shell LiveWIRE
www.shell-livewire.org/
Unlock your potential with this excellent site. Plus financial action planning and a fabulous business encyclopaedia. For 16–30 year olds who want to start and develop their own business

Start-ups
www.startups.co.uk

Job sites

International

www.asia-net.com
Jobs in the Asia–Pacific region, especially Japan, China and Korea

www.asia.hobsons.com
Careers in Asia from Hobsons with regional outlooks

www.blis.org.uk/jobs
BLIS Jobs, a site for people with languages, maintained by CILT, the National Centre for Languages

www.careerseurope.co.uk
Careers Europe, the UK National Resource Centre for international careers information

www.CareerJournalEurope.com
A US site, but lots of useful career tips for everyone.

www.europa.eu.int/eures
EURES, the European job mobility portal

www.gaijinpot.com
The number one site for foreigners in Japan.

www.multilingualvacancies.com
Jobs in Europe using languages

www.monster.co.uk
Lists jobs using languages in the UK and elsewhere

www.lingojobs.com
Jobs for bilingual and multilingual job seekers in the UK and other
European countries

www.prospects.ac.uk
With country specific information

www.reed.co.uk
Lots of graduate vacancies online with plenty of good advice

www.talent4europe.com
A site featuring jobs in all EU countries

www.workinjapan.com
For those of you who would like to work in Japan

www.workpermit.com
Lots of information about immigration and visas worldwide

UK

www.ft.com
Financial Times newspaper

www.timesonline.co.uk
The Times

www.getalife.org.uk
Careers guidance and information for the public sector

www.joslinrowe.co.uk
Joslin Rowe, with lots of opportunities in the financial services
sector, including accountancy, finance and office support. It has

global alliances in Australia, New Zealand, South Africa, Poland and more. It has a Working Worldwide Guide

www.officeteamuk.com
OfficeTeam have offices in the UK, Australia, Canada, New Zealand, plus the USA and various European countries. They place staff in administrative roles including HR, customer services, PA and office manager

www.irecruit.co.uk

www.languagebusiness.co.uk
customer services, IT helpdesk, financial support, administration and secretarial, market research and telemarketing, account management, sales and marketing and data editing, predominantly in London and the Home Counties, but with some opportunities overseas for those of you with language skills

www.people-first.co.uk
recruiting supply chain, multilingual and Japanese speakers

www.naturalbornbillers.co.uk
sales, marketing and customer service for bilingual speakers

www.linguistsdirect.com
jobs in IT and telecommunications

Universities, colleges and schools

These sites will be helpful:

www.jobs.ac.uk
the official recruitment website for staffing in higher education

www.jobs.tes.co.uk

www.eteach.com

Fair trade

Fairtrade Foundation
www.fairtrade.org.uk

Equal Exchange
www.equalexchange.uk.com

Specific help

www.firstimpressions.cm.uk
Image consultantcy

Protecting your creativity

Patent Office
www.patent.gov.uk
For details on how to apply for registration, design, copyright and
trademarks

ACID – Anti Copying in Design
www.acid.uk.com

Institute of Trade Mark Attorneys
www.itma.org.uk

Usability Professionals' Association
www.upassoc.org

Professional organisations and trade associations

The following are examples of professional and trade associations
which relate to business and finance. Many have international links
with their peers abroad, so research their websites thoroughly

Actuaries

Institute of Actuaries
Napier House
4 Worcester Street
Oxford OX1 2AW
Tel: 01865 268 200
www.actuaries.org.uk
institute@actuaries.org.uk
The Highlights of Success as an Actuary available from the Institute
of Actuaries at the above address or by email

Accountancy

Association of Chartered Certified Accountants (ACCA)
2 Central Quay
89 Hydepark Street
Glasgow G3 8BW
Tel: 0141 582 2000
www.accaglobal.com
info@accaglobal.com

Chartered Institute of Management Accountants
26 Chapter Street
London SW1P 4NP
Tel: 0208 849 2251
www.cimaglobal.com

Chartered Institute of Public Finance and Accountancy
3 Robert Street
London WC2N 6RL
Tel: 0207 543 5600
ww.cipfa.org.uk
choices@cipfa.org

Chartered Institute of Taxation
12 Upper Belgrave Street
London SW1X 8BB
Tel: 0208 235 9381
www.tax.org.uk

Institute of Chartered Accountants in England and Wales
PO Box 433
Chartered Accountants' Hall
Moorgate Place
London EC2P 2BJ
Tel: 0207 920 8100
www.icaew.co.uk
careers@icaew.co.uk

Institute of Chartered Accountants of Scotland
CA House
21 Haymarket Yards
Edinburgh EH12 5BH
Tel: 0131 347 0100
www.icas.org.uk
coeducation@icas.org.uk

Institute of Internal Auditors
13 Abbeville Mews
88 Clapham Park Road
London SW4 7BX
Tel: 0207 498 0101
www.iia.org.uk
info@iia.org.uk

Administration/Secretarial

Company Secretary

Institute of Chartered Secretaries and Administrators
16 Park Crescent
London W1B 1AH
Tel: 0207 580 4741
www.icsa.org.uk

Council for Administration
6 Graphite Square
Vauxhall Walk
London SE11 5EE
Tel: 0207 091 9620
www.cfa.uk.com
www.breakinto.biz
Information on careers in administration

Personal assistant

Institute of Qualified Professional Secretaries
Suite 464
24–28 St Leonard's Road
Windsor
Berks SL4 3BB
Tel: 0844 8000 182

Association of Medical Secretaries, Practice Managers, Administrators and Receptionists (AMSPAR)
Tavistock House North
Tavistock Square
London WC1H 9LN
www.amspar.co.uk

Institute of Business Administration and Management
16 Park Crescent
London W1B 1AH
Tel: 0207 580 4741
www.ibam.org.uk
info@ibam.org.uk

Advertising

Advertising Association
7th Floor North
Artillery House
11–19 Artillery Row
London SW1P 1RT
Tel: 0207 340 1100
www.adassoc.org.uk
aa@adassoc.org.uk
The AA's careers guide Getting into Advertising can be down-loaded from the website

Institute of Practitioners in Advertising
44 Belgrave Square
London SW1X 8QS
Tel: 0207 235 7020
www.ipa.co.uk

Banking/Building societies

Bank of England
www.bankofengland.co.uk
Access The City Handbook, available on the Internet. It has information on over 150 financial organisations, mostly in the City of London

Chartered Institute of Bankers in Scotland
Drumsheugh House
386 Drumsheugh Gardens
Edinburgh EH3 7SW
Tel: 0131 473 7777
www.ciobs.org.uk

London Investment Banking Association
6 Frederick's Place
London WC2R 8BT
Tel: 0207 796 3606
www.liba.org.uk

Building Societies Association
3 Savile Row
London W1S 3PB
Tel: 0207 437 0655
www.bsa.org.uk

Institute of Financial Services
IFS House
4–9 Burgate Lane
Canterbury
Kent CR1 2XJ
Tel: 01227 818 609
www.ifslearning.com
institute@ifs.learning.com

Call centres

Call Centre Management Association UK
International House
174 Three Bridges Road
Crawley
West Sussex RH10 1LE
Tel: 01293 538 400
www.ccma.org.uk
membership@ccma.org.uk

Call Centre Association
20 Newton Place
Glasgow G3 7PY
Tel: 0141 564 9010
www.cca.org.uk
cca@cca.org.uk

Charities/Voluntary sector

Working For A Charity
NCVO
Regent's Wharf
8 All Saints Street
London N1 9RL
Tel: 0207 520 2512
Fax: 0207 713 6300
www.wfac.org.uk

Economists

Society of Business Economics
Dean House
Vernham Dean
Andover
Hants SP11 0JZ
Tel: 01264 737552
www.sbe.co.uk

HM Treasury
Correspondence and Enquiry Unit
2/W1
HM Treasury
1 Horse Guards Road
London SW1A 2HQ
Tel: 0207 270 4558
www.hm-treasury.gov.uk/careers

Estate agents

National Association of Estate Agents
Arbon House
21 Jury Street
Warwick CV34 4EH
Tel: 01926 496 800
www.naea.co.uk
info@naea.co.uk

Ethical and socially/environmentally responsible careers

www.peopleandplanet.org
Find a socially and envrionmentally responsible career
www.ethicalcareersguide.co.uk
The essential guide to careers in charity, development, social enterprise and voluntary organisations and more. You can order your copy online

Event, exhibition and conference organisation

Association for Conferences and Events
ACE International
Riverside House
High Street
Huntingdon
Cambridgeshire PE18 6SG
Tel: 01480 457 595
www.martex.co.uk/ace
ace@martex.co.uk

Association of Exhibition Organisers
119 High Street
Berkhamsted
Hertfordshire HP4 2DJ
Tel: 01442 873 331
www.aeo.org.uk
info@aeo.org.uk

Financial services

Association of Independent Financial Advisers
Austin Friars House
2–6 Austin Friars
London EC2N 2HD
Tel: 0207 628 1287
www.aifa.net

Financial Services Skills Council
51 Gresham Street
London EC2V 7HQ
Tel: 0207 216 7366
www.fssc.org.uk

Institute of Financial Planning
Whitefriars Centre
Lewins Mead
Bristol BS1 2NT
Tel: 0117 945 2470
www.financialplanning.org.uk

Society of Financial Advisers
20 Aldermanbury
London EC2V 7HY
Tel: 0208 530 0852
www.sofa.org
info@sofa.org

UK Society of Investment Professionals
90 Basinghall Street
London EC2V 5AY
Tel: 0207 796 3000
www.uksip.org
uksipstaff@uksip.org

Fundraising

Institute of Fundraising
Park Place
12 Lawn Lane
London SW8 1UD
Tel: 0207 840 1000
www.institute-of-fundraising.org.uk

Healthcare management

Institute of Healthcare Management
18–21 Morley St
London SE1 7QZ
Tel: 0207 620 1030
www.ihm.org.uk

Housing

Chartered Institute of Housing
Octavia House
Westwood Business Park
Westwood Way
Coventry CV4 8JP
Tel: 024 7685 1700
www.cih.org
careers@cih.org

Human resources/Personnel

Chartered Institute of Personnel and Development
151 The Broadway
London SW19 1JQ
Tel: 0208 612 6200
www.cipd.co.uk
cipd@cipd.co.uk

Insurance

Chartered Insurance Institute
Training Advisory Services
42–48 High Road
South Woodford
London E18 2JP
Tel: 0208 989 8464
www.cii.co.uk
customer.serv@cii.co.uk

Chartered Institute of Loss Adjusters
Peninsular House
36 Monument Street
London EC3R 9LJ
Tel: 0207 337 9960
www.cila.co.uk
info@cila.co.uk

General Insurance Standards Council
110 Cannon Street
London EC4N 6EU
Tel: 0207 648 7800
www.gisc.co.uk

Law

Faculty of Advocates
11 Parliament Square
Edinburgh EH1 1RF
Tel: 0131 226 5017
www.advocates.org.uk

Bar Council
289–293 High Holborn
London WC1V 7HZ
Tel: 0207 242 0082
www.barcouncil.org.uk
www.legaleducation.org.uk
Details of education and training at the Bar

Institute of Legal Executives
Kempston Manor
Kempston
Bedford MK42 7AB
Tel: 01234 841000
www.ilex.org.uk
info@ilex.org.uk

Law Society
113 Chancery Lane
London WC2A 1PL
Tel: 01527 504423 (for information on becoming a solicitor)
www.lawsociety.org.uk
legaled@lawsociety.org.uk

Law Society of Scotland
26 Drumsheugh Gardens
Edinburgh EH3 7YR
Tel: 0131 226 7411
www.lawscot.org.uk

Notaries Society
PO Box 226
Melton
Woodbridge
Suffolk IP12 1DN
www.thenotariessociety.org.uk
admin@thenotariessociety.org.uk

Leisure/Recreation

Fitness Industry Association
4th Floor
61 Southwark Street
London SE1 0HL
Tel: 0207 202 4700
www.fia.org.uk
info@fia.org.uk

Institute of Leisure and Amenity Management
ILAM House
Lower Basildon
Reading
Berkshire RG8 9NE
Tel: 01491 874 800
www.ilam.co.uk
info@ilam.co.uk

Institute of Sport and Recreation Management
Sir John Beckwith Centre for Sport
Loughborough University
Loughborough LE11 3TU
Tel: 01509 226474
www.isrm.co.uk
info@isrm.co.uk

Management consultancy

Institute of Management Consultancy
3rd Floor, 17–18 Hayward's Place
London EC1R 0EQ
Tel: 0207 566 5220
www.imc.co.uk
consult@imc.co.uk

Institute of Management Services
Brooke House
24 Dan Street
Lichfield
Staffordshire WS13 6AB
Tel: 01543 266 909
ww.ims-productivity.com

Management Consultancies Association
49 Whitehall
London SW1A 2BX
Tel: 0207 321 3990
www.mca.org.uk
The website has an 'inside careers' guide you can download

Marketing

CAM Foundation Ltd
(Communications and Marketing Education Foundation Ltd)
Moor Hall
Cookham
Maidenhead
Berks SL6 9QH
Tel: 01628 427 120
www.camfoundation.com
info@camfoundation.com

Chartered Institute of Marketing
Moor Hall
Cookham
Maidenhead
Berkshire SL6 9QH
Tel: 01628 427 500
www.cim.co.uk

Direct Marketing Association
DMA House
70 Margaret Street
London W1W 8SS
Tel: 0207 201 3300
www.dma.org.uk

Managing and Marketing Sales Association
PO Box 11
Sandbach
Cheshire CW11 3GE
Tel: 01270 526 339
www.mamsasbp.com
mamsa@mamsasbp.com

Public relations

Chartered Institute of Public Relations
3 St James's Square
London sW1Y4JR
Tel: 0207 766 3333
www.ipr.org.uk

Public Relations Consultants Association
Willow House
Willow Place
London SW1P 1JH
Tel: 0207 233 6026
www.prca.org.uk

Purchasing and supply

Chartered Institute of Purchasing and Supply
Easton House
Easton on the Hill
Stamford
Leicestershire PE9 3NZ
Tel: 01780 756 777
www.cips.org

Recruitment

Recruitment and Employment Confederation
36–38 Mortimer Street
London W1W 7RG
Tel: 0207 462 3260
www.rec.uk.com

Retail

Skillsmart Retail Ltd
The Retail Sector Skills Council
40 Duke Street
London W1A 1AB
Tel: 0207 399 3450
www.skillsmart.com

Risk and safety management

International Institute of Risk and Safety Management
Suite 7a
77 Fulham Palace Road
London W6 8TA
Tel: 0208 741 9100
www.iirsm.org
info@iirsm.org

Sales

Institute of Sales Promotion
Arena House
66–68 Pentonville Road
London N1 9HS
Tel: 0207 837 5340
www.isp.org.uk

Institute of Sales and Marketing Management
Harrier Court
Lower Woodside
Bedfordshire LU1 4DQ
Tel: 01582 840001
www.ismm.co.uk

Statisticians

Royal Statistical Society
12 Errol Street
London EC1Y 8LX
Tel: 0207 638 8998
www.rss.org.uk
rss@rss.org.uk

Stockbrokers

Securities and Investment Institute
Centurion House
24 Monument Street
London EC3R 8AQ
Tel: 0207 645 0600
www.securities-institute.org.uk
info@securities-institute.org.uk

Shipbroking

Baltic Exchange
38 St Mary's Axe
London EC3A 8BH
Tel: 0207 623 5501
www.balticexchange.com

Institute of Chartered Shipbrokers
85 Gracechurch Street
London EC3V 0AA
Tel: 0207 623 1111
www.ics.org.uk
info@ics.org.uk

Tourism and hospitality

Confederation of Tourism, Hotel and Catering Management
118–120 Great Titchfield Street
London W1W 6SS
Tel: 0207 612 0170
www.cthcm.com
info@cthcm.com

Hotel and Catering International Management Association
Trinity Court
34 West Street
Sutton
Surrey SM1 1SH
Tel: 0208 661 4900
www.hcima.org.uk

Institute of Travel and Tourism
PO Box 217
Ware
Herts SG12 8WY
Tel: 0870 770 7960
www.itt.co.uk

Transport

British International Freight Association
Institute of Freight Forwarders
Redfern House
Browells Lane
Feltham
Middlesex TW13 7EP
Tel: 0208 844 2266
www.bifa.org
bifa@bifa.org

Institute of Transport Administrators
IoTA House
7B St Leonards Road
Horsham
West Sussex RH13 6EH
Tel: 01403 242 412
www.iota.org.uk

The Chartered Institute of Logistics and Transport
Logistics and Transport Centre
Earlstreets Court
Earlstreets Road
Corby
Northants NN17 4AX
Tel: 01536 740104
www.ciltuk.org.uk

UK Civil Service

www.civilservice.gov.uk/careers
access to all departments via the Recruitment Gateway

www.capitaras.co.uk
jobs in the Civil Service

www.faststream.gov.uk
information about the fast stream development programme

www.euro-staff.gov.uk
information about jobs in Europe

NHS careers

Careers helpline
0845 6060 655

www.nhscareers.nhs.uk

www.futureleaders.nhs.uk
graduate management training

Local government

www.LGcareers.com
careers information

www.LGjobs.com
current job vacancies